Find Your Frame

Find Your Frame

A street
photography
masterclass

Craig Whitehead

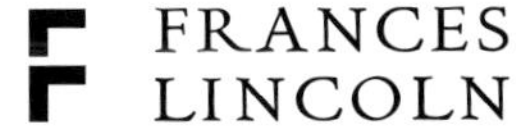

FRANCES LINCOLN

Contents

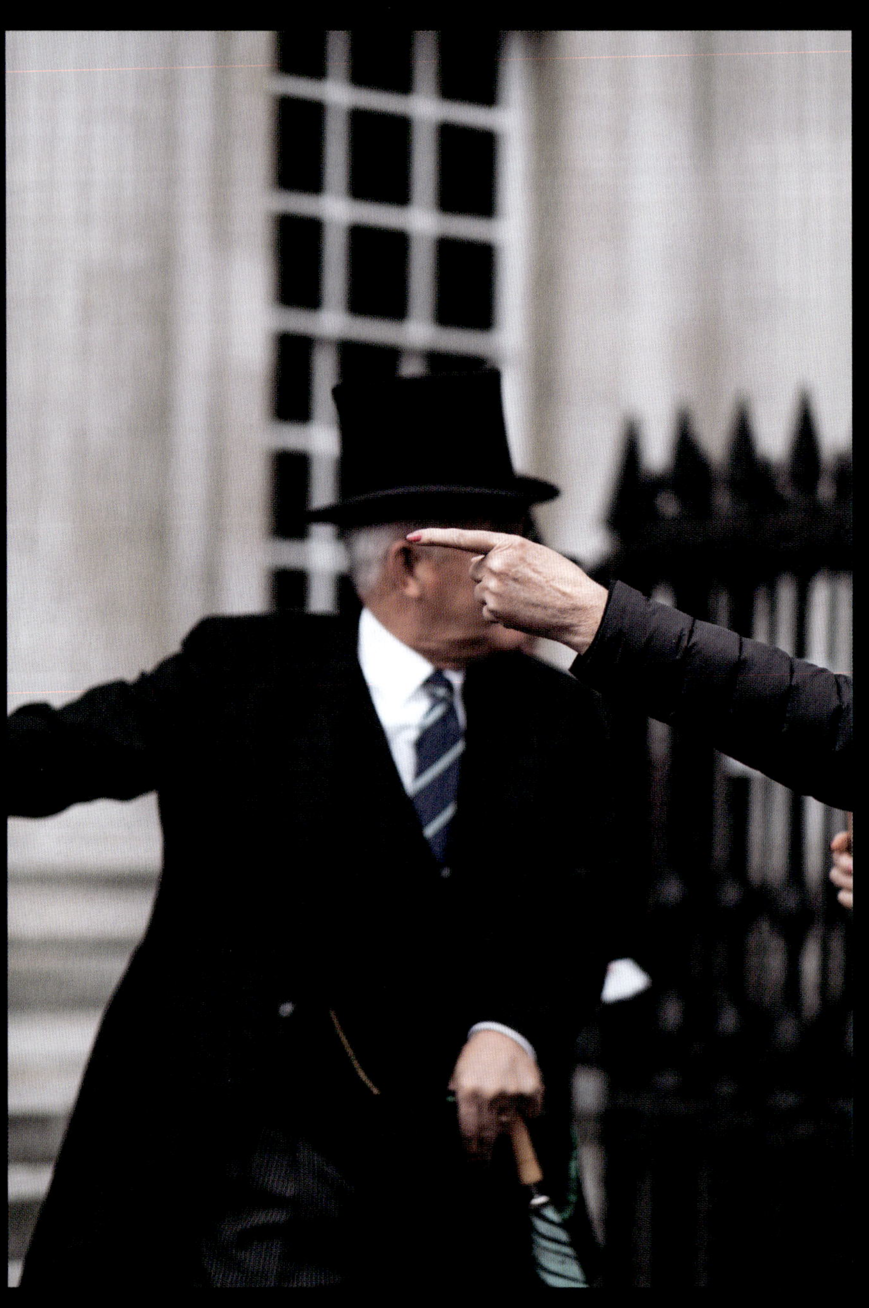

Foreword

By Kai Wong

What a fantastic honour it is to be given this opportunity to write a foreword for a book written by my friend and fellow photographer, Craig Whitehead, who I have known for years and with whom I have shot many a street photo, sometimes risking life and limb – you'd be surprised at the damage a load of projectile Brussel sprouts can do – just to get that elusive street shot. He is a great guy and an even better photographer, as his photos bear testament. Take a look at his images and you will soon get a sense of his unique style and identity, which have become somewhat of a rarity in the age of social media where the quest for success – interactions, likes and follows – has often come at the expense of originality.

Craig certainly sees the world differently. He takes elements that are familiar and composes them in a refreshingly new way that is a visual feast for the eyes – his work is part-conventional street photography, part-abstract art, part-surrealism, part 'I-don't-know-what-label-to-put-on-it-but-it's-really-rather-good'. He is a gifted photographer who is technically proficient, yet has an artistic way of using the frame to put together lines and shapes in a geometrically pleasing manner. The little details to which Craig pays attention will make you want to come back for more. His images have depth; they are more than just pretty, perfectly composed pictures. You are not just looking at the photo, you are also taking a peek into the mind of Craig Whitehead.

Photography like this doesn't come from being a casual snapper, and Craig is certainly dedicated to his craft. I first met him on the street, when he was busy taking photos, and I always had a knack of bumping into him whenever he was doing so. When we did meet up, it was to get busy with taking street photos and we only ever talked about street photography. I can't tell you what his favourite colour is or who his favourite *Ghostbuster* is, but what I can tell you is that, apart from taking amazing images, Craig is wonderfully articulate about his approach to taking street photos, which is always insightful and inspiring for photographers of any proficiency to elevate their own work to another level.

Even if you don't have the benefit of running into him and marvelling at his work being made live, you have the good fortune of having this lovely book, filled with all his luscious photos and inspiring thoughts about street photography, with which to treat your eyes and mind. Enjoy!

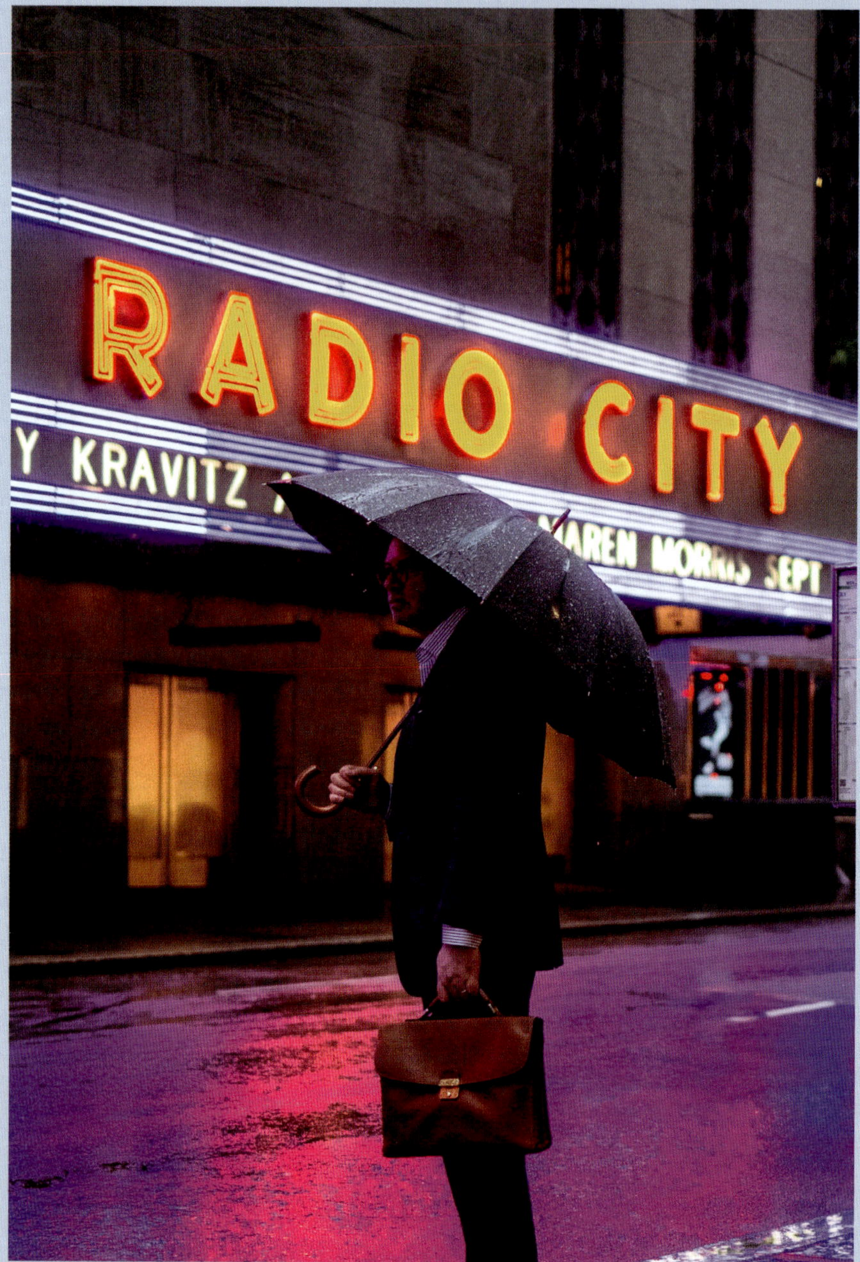

The street is only ever the starting point. It's up to you where to go from there.
New York, 2019

1

Street your way

Look beyond the obvious – street photography is what you make it

I f someone asked you to define street photography, what would you say? The most obvious answer is: photography that takes place in the street. That's a start, though you could equally be photographing scenes in a park or a café, on the London Underground or through a bus window, and I believe it would still count. You'll find all sorts of different guides or rules for being a street photographer, in books like this or in online articles. But the truth is, if you really want to be thought of as one, you just need to take candid photographs in public.

For a picture to be 'candid', it has to represent a situation as it unfolded in reality, unposed and unstaged. You can't direct the people in the shot to stand in a particular way and you can't set things up, but you can engineer situations in other, subtle ways. My own movements and actions will have an impact on the frame I capture. If I want someone staring into the lens, for example, I might

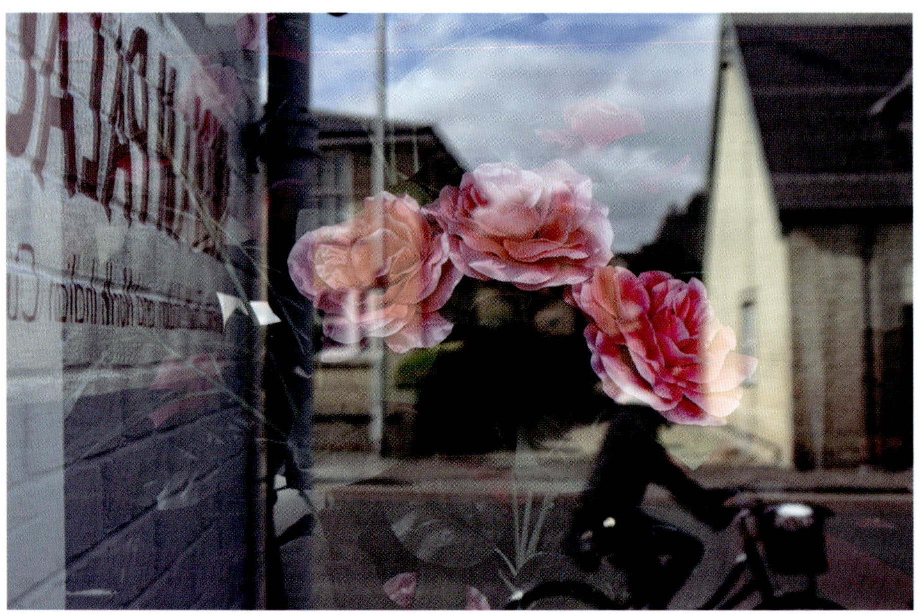

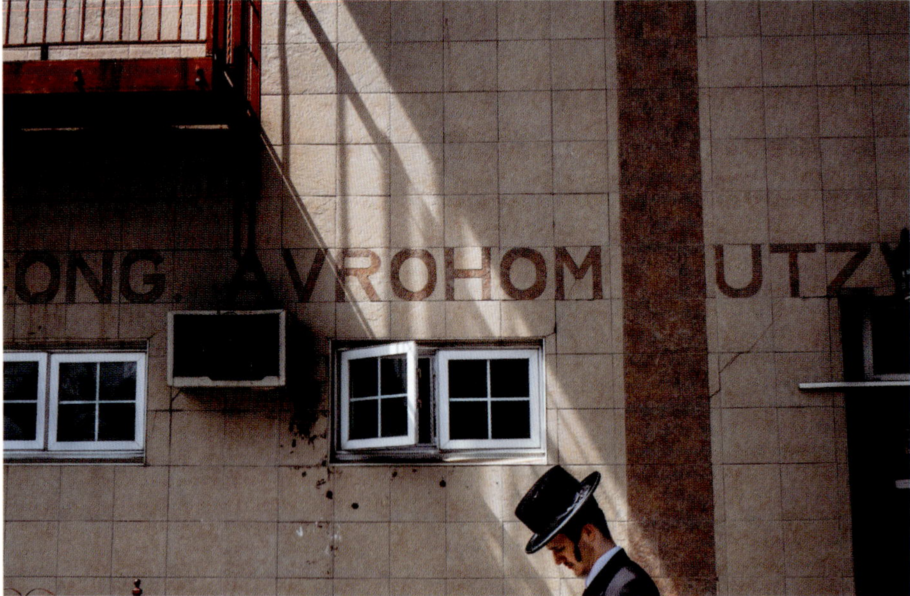

The images I shoot don't look like classic, fast-paced street photography.
ABOVE Cambridge, 2020
BELOW New York, 2018

take a step towards them or ostentatiously lift up my camera. Of course, there are certain traditions that people associate with street photography. The generation of postwar photographers who pioneered the genre would shoot black-and-white images on a 35mm lens, and that has shaped a perception of what street photography should look like – dynamic images portraying fleeting moments of fast-moving human interaction.

'For a picture to be "candid", it has to represent a situation as it unfolded in reality, unposed and unstaged.'

Fast forward to now and street photography is hugely influenced by social media. That's problematic because it's quite circular, like a feedback loop where everyone's prompted by the same things. Another common misconception is that, for many, street photography is synonymous with photographs of people. While those early trailblazers might have focused mainly on people, some of the biggest names among the all-time greats would simply photograph things on the street that caught their eye – a cup in a certain shade of red that they just instinctively liked. They documented what was around them, whatever it was. Such images aren't as popular on social media, so contemporary photographers tend to avoid them and that's a shame.

I became a street photographer out of necessity. When I began taking pictures seriously, I was squeezing in shoots before shifts at work or during breaks, so I needed to make the time count. I'd head out and hit the streets around where I was. My eye soon acclimatised to this space. I became familiar with its interesting spots, got a feel for its rhythms, the way that light would fall at different times. Gradually, I fell in step with the city. Now it's like a switch I can't turn off. Cutting my teeth as a street photographer in this way reminded me of my 17 years spent rollerblading. That taught me how to read the city. It is also the reason I got my first camera, as a tool to document what my friends and I were doing. It's no coincidence that many of my fellow street photographers, including Matt Stuart, were once skaters.

At first, I did street photography in the way I thought I should and that was in the style of Bruce Gilden, the first street photographer whose work I came across. I got right into people's faces, inches from the action, using a wide-angle lens and seeking out random encounters between city dwellers. Over time, though, I changed my approach. I discovered a school of street photographers that chimed with my way of seeing the world – people like the legendary Saul Leiter and Ernst Haas, who used colour, light and form to create abstracted works which just happened to be in the street. At this point, I stopped seeking out faces and moved to using longer lenses; working with lenses between 85 and 135mm allowed me to hone right in on details, until I felt the time had come to challenge myself by trying something wider again. I like to keep things fresh.

My background is in illustration and it was only about three years ago that I began to connect the dots between that and my approach to street photography. In the end, that's why I came to love the work of the more painterly street photographers, because their inspirations were exactly the same as mine. They loved light, texture, layering and colour. I'm obsessed with colour, as anyone who's seen much of my work would tell you, but really it comes down to interesting composition. I don't do much post-processing, but I also don't have a problem with cropping to get the composition I'm after. Beyond the basic rule of candid photography, you can create your own way of working and that will contribute to a style that is uniquely yours.

Remember: to be a great street photographer, don't allow yourself to be limited or weighed down by the label. Increasingly, I try not to pigeonhole myself, instead being open to creativity and seeing where that takes me. In this book, you can join me on that journey.

'Create your own way
of working and that
will contribute to a style
that is uniquely yours.'

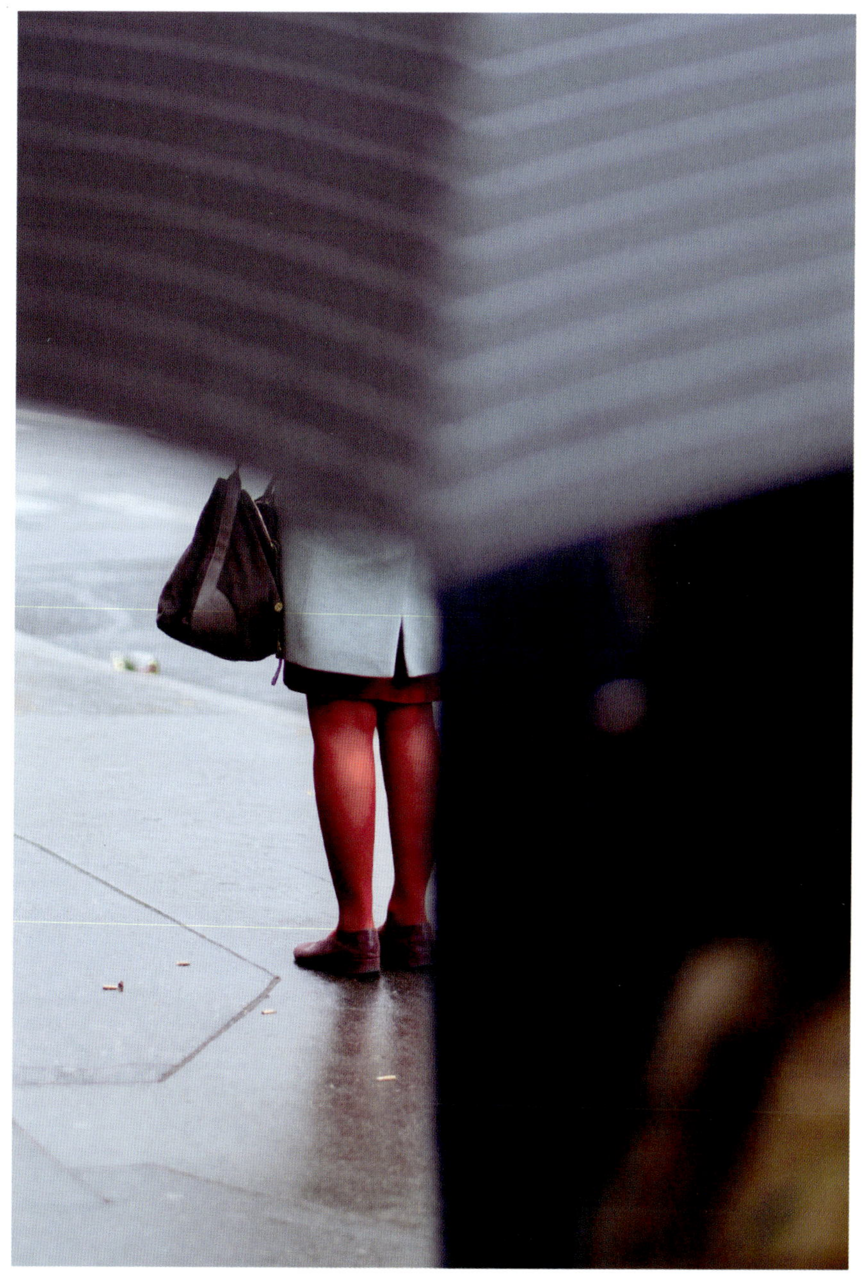

I compose using bold colours and strong shapes, rather than seeking random moments.
Paris, 2018

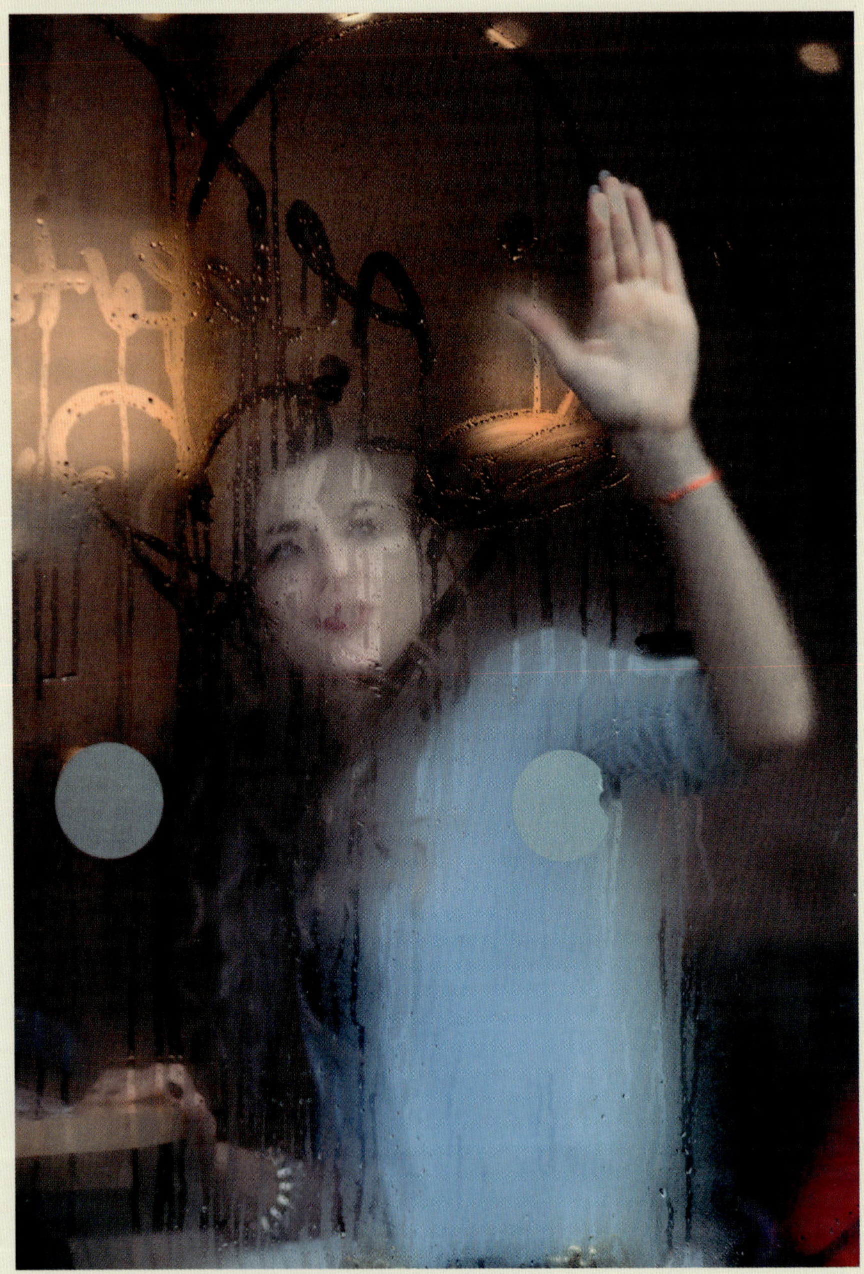

Images like this appear before your eyes – once you know the right places to look.
London, 2018

2

Find your tribe

Test out different street photography styles and pick one that suits

Like so many other rookie street photographers before and after me, I started out with a fixed idea in my head of what street photography was about. All I knew was the brash, in-your-face style of New Yorkers like Bruce Gilden. I had a basic kit – a Fuji camera body and a 12mm Samyang Optics lens – and that shaped how I worked initially. Although I tend not to shoot like that now, working with a wide-angle lens forced me to figure out how to engineer myself into a position that was 50cm (20in) away from someone to get a shot – a skill that I still find useful from time to time.

As I got deeper into street photography, I learned that there are primarily two types of street photographer, known in the game as 'hunters' and 'fishers'. The up-close, fast-paced street photographers are the hunters; they pound the pavements in search of people doing odd things to give interest to their images. Take Gilden, who is completely obsessed with characters, or Joel

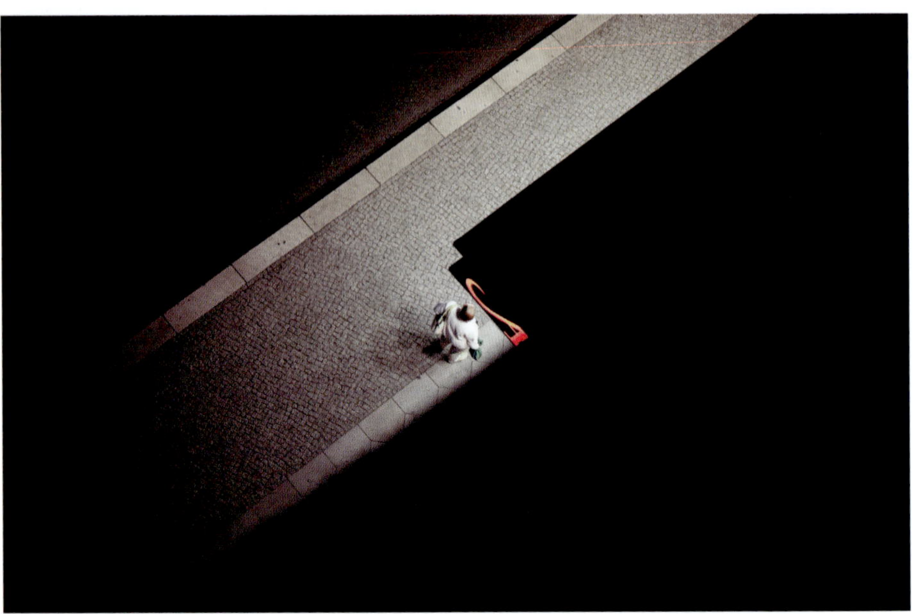

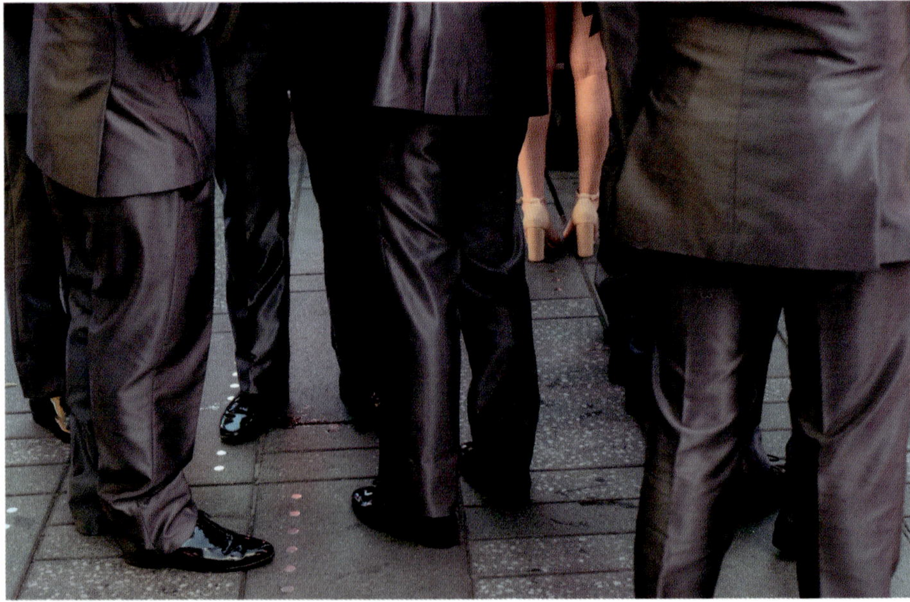

Here, humans aren't the primary focus – I see them more as compositional elements.
ABOVE Berlin, 2018
BELOW New York, 2018

Meyerowitz, for example. Meyerowitz goes out looking for unrepeatable moments. He's not seeking abstract frames devoid of human figures, he's thinking people first and then composing around them. I tend to work the other way around. I'm more of a fisher. I work more slowly, waiting for the right composition to bite; people are usually incidental – the final element in my frame, rather than the starting point.

'The more you explore, the faster you will find a style that really resonates with you.'

I'm not sure where this comes from, but I think it's deeply rooted in me. If there's a group conversation going on, I'm not looking at people's faces, but just seeing everything that's going on around them. I've always been like that and because I've spent my whole life not really making eye contact, I'm just not so bothered by it. I'm asking, what are their hands doing and why? What shoes are they wearing? I understand the psychology of why faces pull people into an image, and I know how to play with that, using elements of faces within advertising to force a viewer to take a certain route through a shot, but what seizes my attention when I'm out in the street is probably not the same as it is for most people.

Familiarize yourself with the history of street photography to find where your own interests lie. Go to museums and look at how artists used light and shadow in the past, check out what contemporary photographers are doing by going to gallery shows, immerse yourself in photo books and websites. Dig around. Russian photographer Gueorgui Pinkhassov makes incredible, high-contrast, saturated images, brilliant silhouettes, but there's not much of his work out there. It turns out Pinterest is the best place to see it.

To understand how these images arise from a particular way of working, nothing beats watching street photographers in action. YouTube and other platforms are full of footage dating back decades where you can see legends of street photography practise their craft – it's an absolutely vital education in the early days. You might watch some of these videos and think, 'Wow, I love that' or you might conclude that it's definitely not your thing, which might lead you down a different path. The more you explore, the faster you will find a style that really resonates with you. I first came across the more painterly approach to street photography that I favour through American photographer and filmmaker Ted Forbes, who runs an excellent YouTube channel called The Art of Photography.

I stumbled across a couple of names – people like Saul Leiter and Ernst Haas – and then went on a mission to find all the content I possibly could about them and to see everything they'd done. There's a documentary by Thomas Leach called *In No Great Hurry: 13 Lessons with Saul Leiter*, which came out in 2013, the year Leiter died. There are also plenty of videos of people talking about Leiter's work and how it inspired them, but there is not too much content available that shows these photographers actually out shooting and discussing their own processes. The hunter's outgoing personality lends itself to that, but this is not the case for the more introverted, painterly type. Another photographer I admire, although he's not strictly a street photographer, is Jack Davison, but I've only found one interview with him talking about how he works.

Leiter and Haas are very much in the same camp. They are painters who just happened to use a camera. In fact, Leiter always wanted to be a painter and he didn't really understand why people cared about his photography the way they did, even towards the end of his career when he started to get more recognition. I suspect he was just criminally humble. What I love about the work of Leiter and Haas is that it can show you something in a way you have never seen it before. I like to be confused by an image – there's real magic in that. I want to be intrigued by what it is and how it's made.

Don't confine yourself to one genre. Street photography, landscape photography, fashion – they all inform each other. If you draw on influences from elsewhere, you'll find your own twist, which will make your work stand out. William Klein and Leiter both took on assignments for *Harper's Bazaar* and when you look back through the latter's archive in particular, you can't always tell whether what you're looking at is staged or not. In the end it doesn't matter – it's just a beautiful image. It's not always obvious how inspiration filters through to your own work. Undeniably, there will sometimes be a scene or moment that you have to capture because you know it reminds you of something. The rest of the time, however, it all happens within your subconscious.

> **'I like to be confused by an image – there's real magic in that.'**

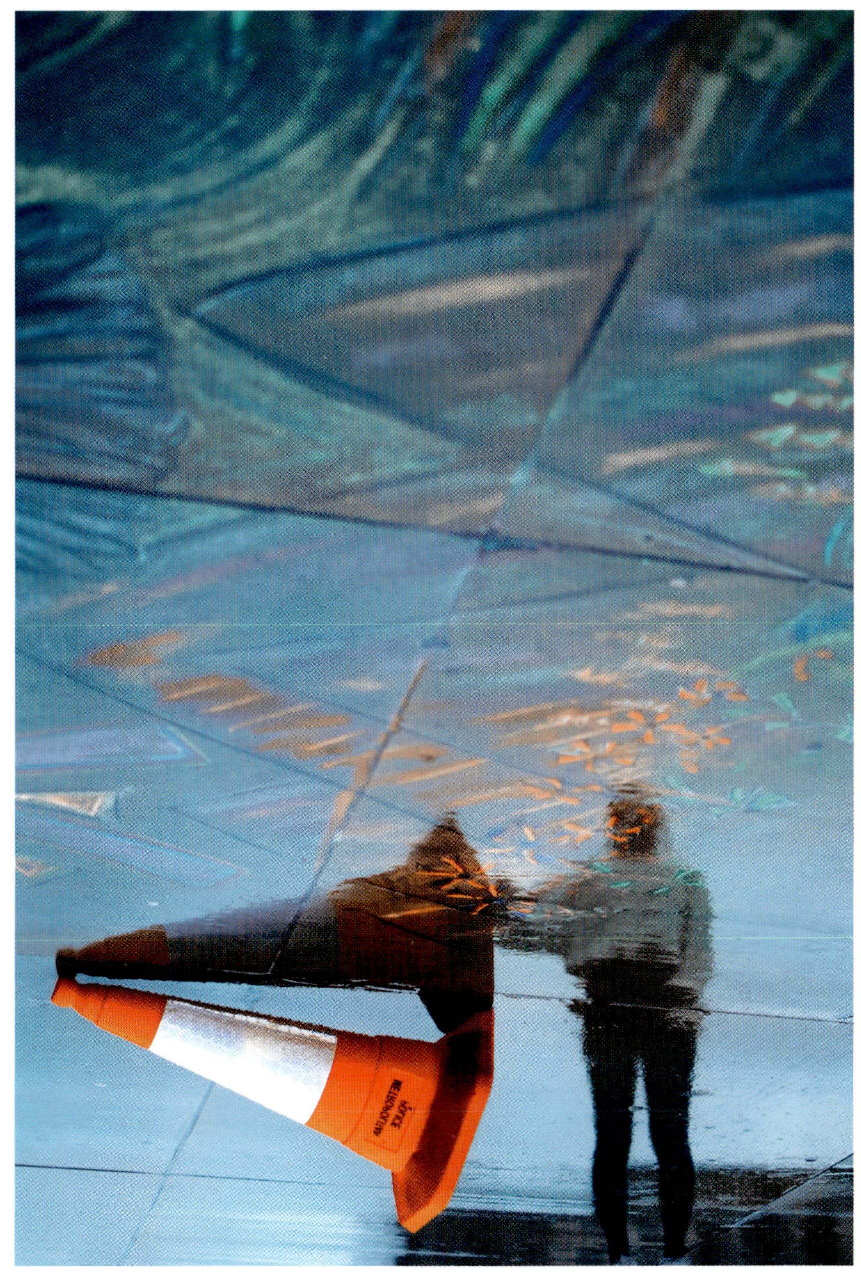

Reflective surfaces like these are great for getting your viewers to do a double-take.
ABOVE London, 2018
OVERLEAF New York, 2018

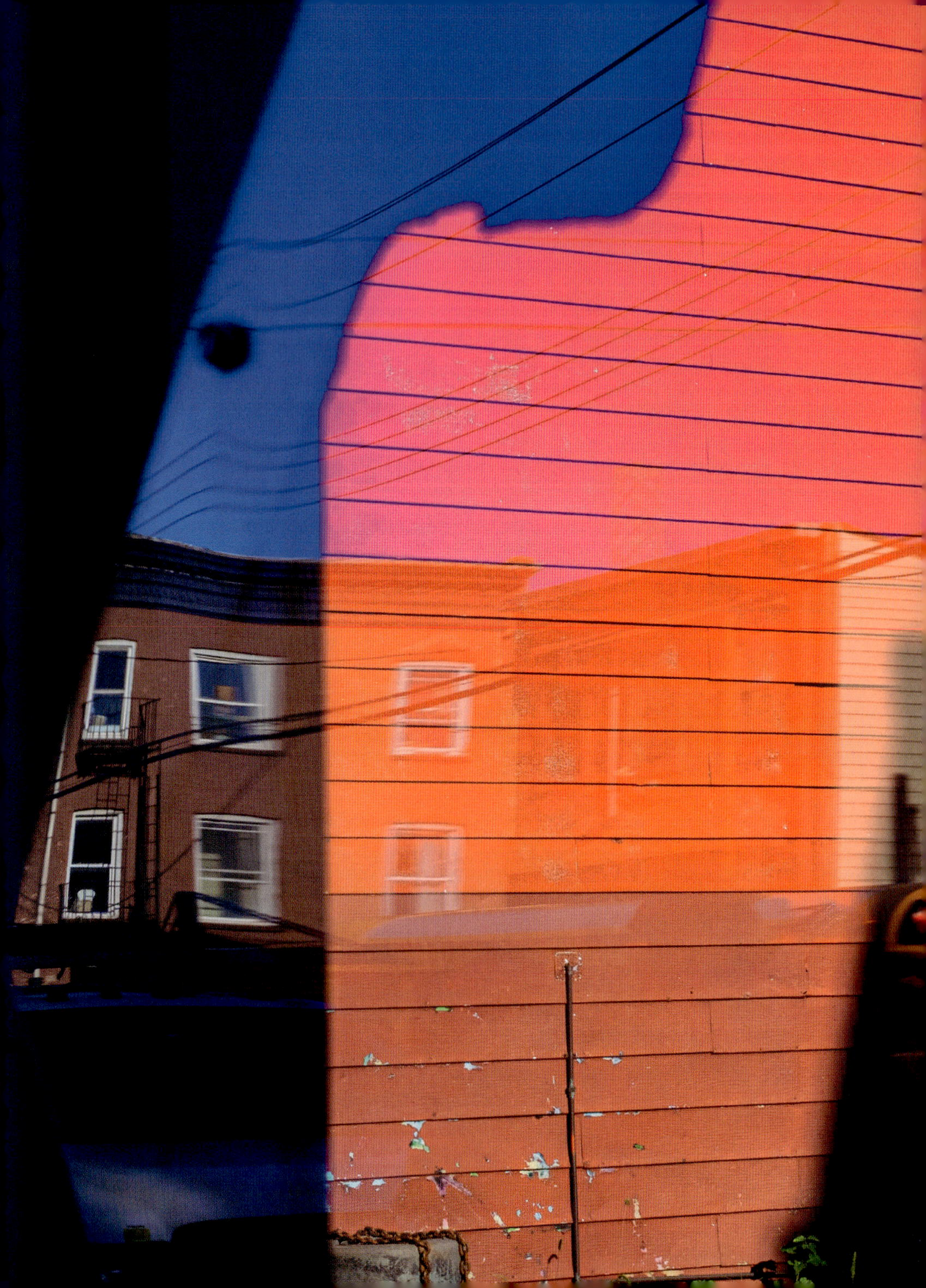

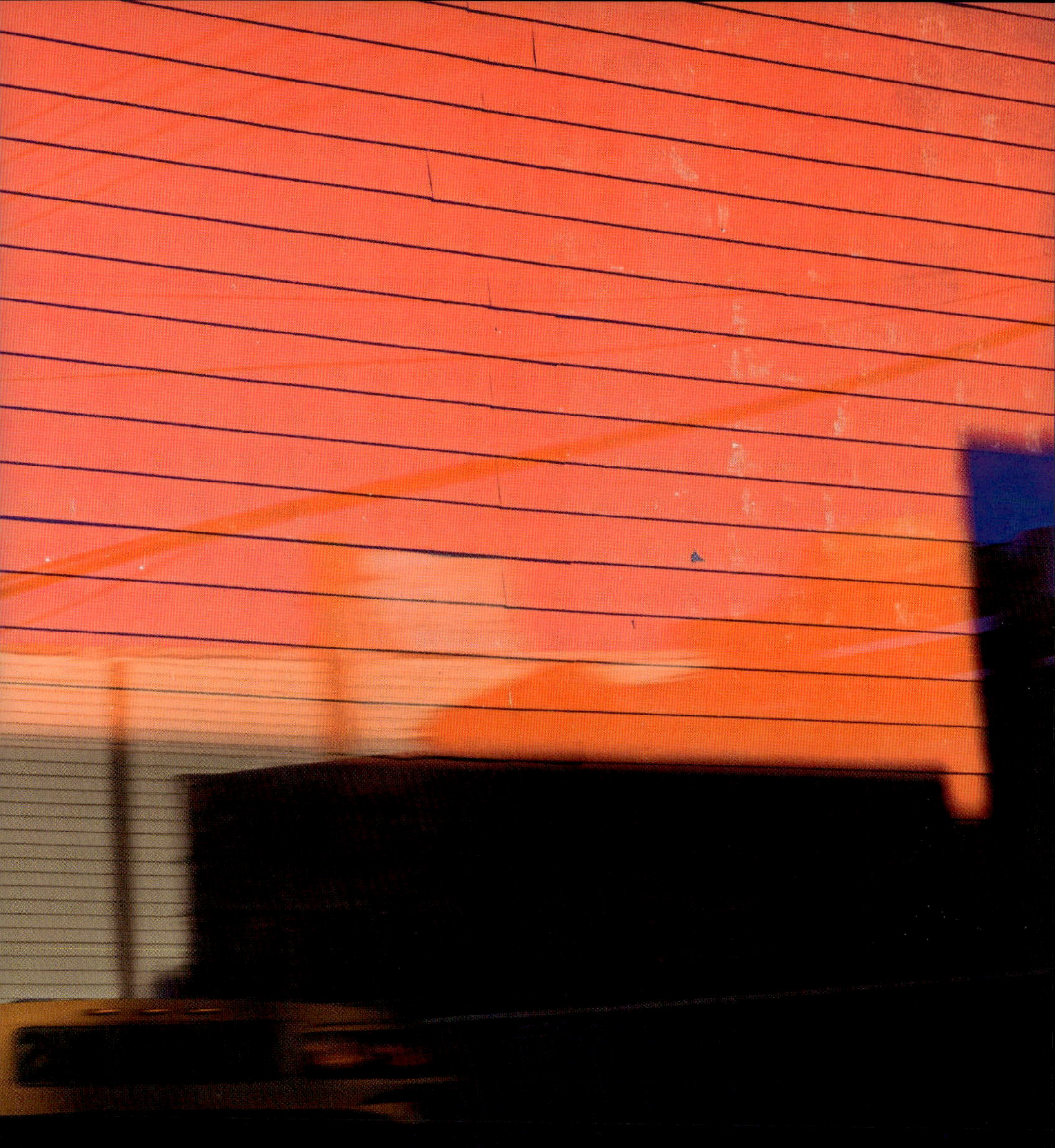

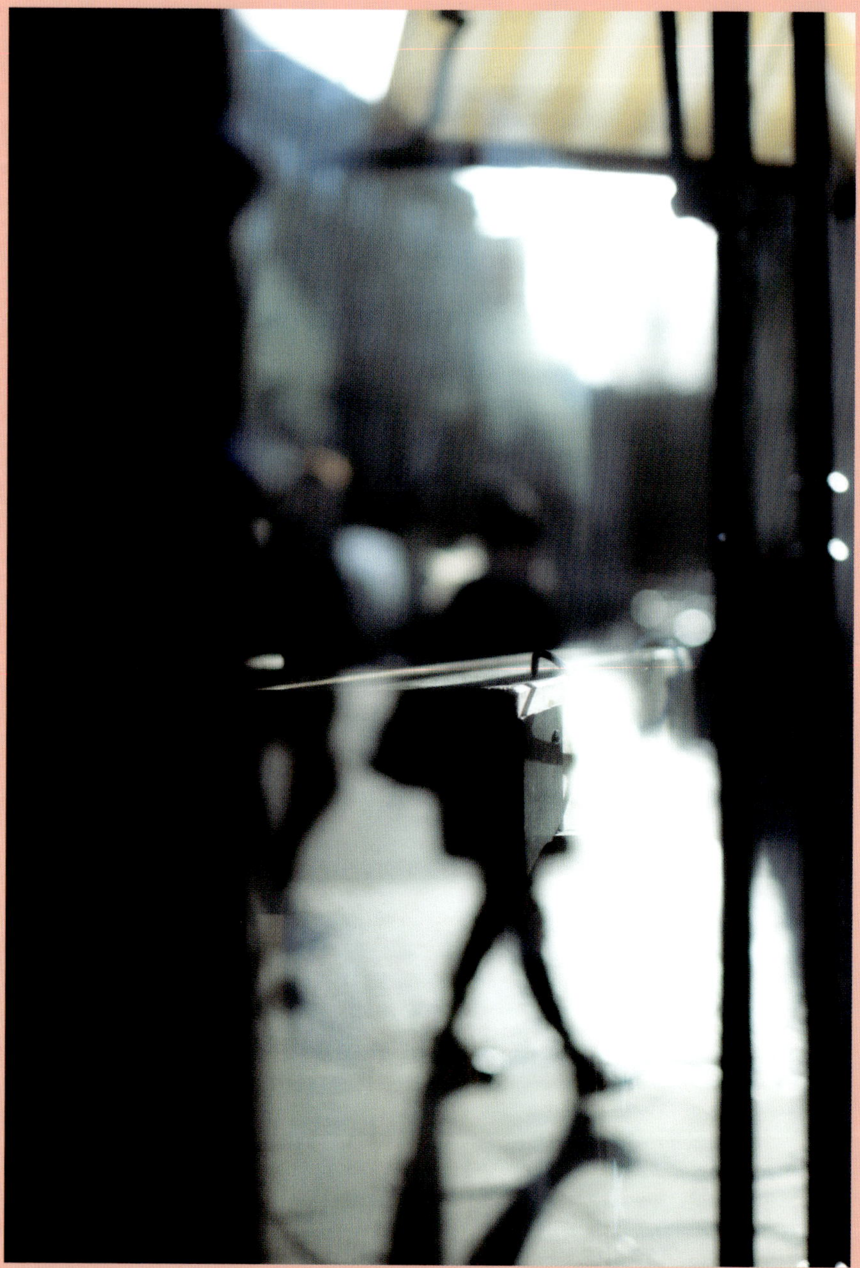

Familiarity with your kit means you can react to fleeting light moments like this.
Cambridge, 2019

Make kit count

All you need is a camera – but one that you know inside out and back to front

'll let you into a secret. What you shoot with doesn't really matter. You can take mind-blowing street photography with the smartphone you carry around every day in your pocket, or, for that matter, with a cheap toy camera. In 2019, I hit the streets of London with photography YouTuber Kai Wong, who had a challenge for me: what kind of photographs could I produce using a *Star Wars* branded camera shaped like a Storm Trooper's head and marketed to four-year-old kids in place of my then usual Fujifilm X-Pro2? It was the ultimate test. How dependent are my photographic skills on the kit I use? Luckily, I did all right.

Of course, using a basic camera or a smartphone places limitations on what you can do. If you want to create certain effects, having the ability to change your lens has an impact, but if you just want to make images that look good, the most important thing is to understand the functional possibilities and constraints of your

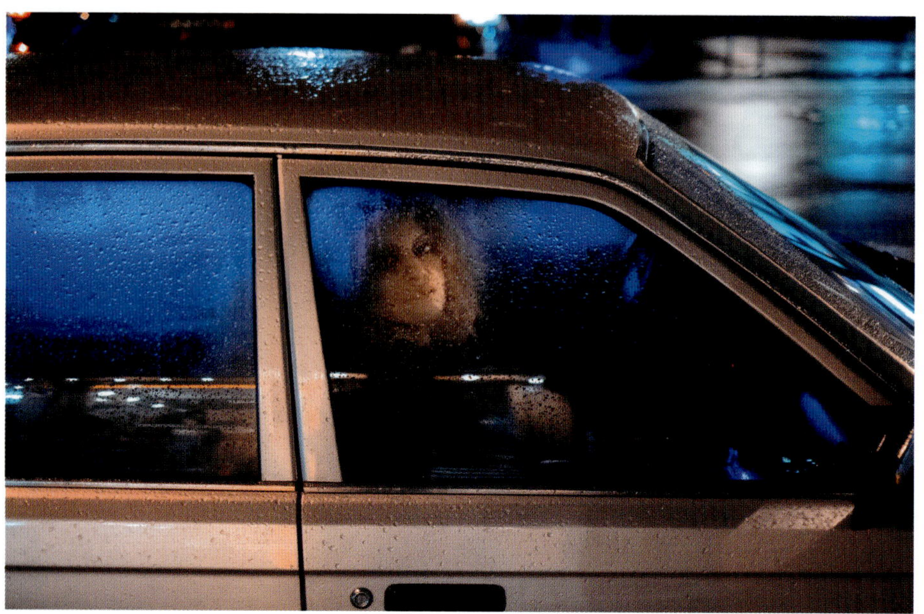

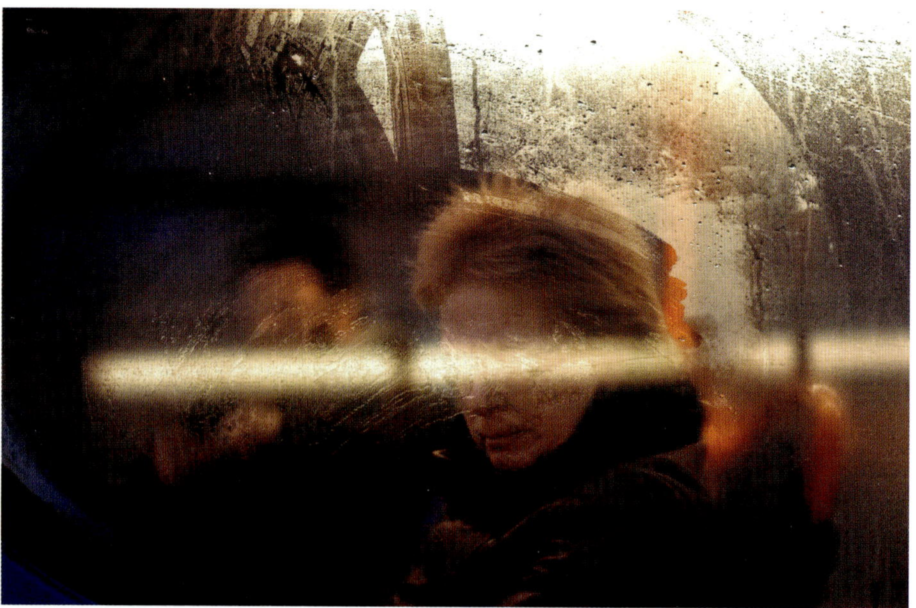

By excluding the wider scene from the frame, your images could be shot anywhere.
ABOVE New York, 2018
BELOW Cambridge, 2018

equipment, whatever they may be – the toy camera, for example, suffered from an irritating shutter lag and the image resolution was a mere two megapixels. The only way you can achieve this is by spending hours and hours out shooting. Once you have done that, and seen how the camera reacts in different situations, using it becomes instinctive. It feels like an extension of your body.

'Once you have seen how the camera reacts in different situations, using it becomes instinctive. It feels like an extension of your body.'

As with almost any aspect of life today, people are obsessed with novelty. They think they have to rush out and buy the latest must-have clothes when they could just buy something second-hand and get it tailored. You should always try to make better use of the things you have. It's just that advertising exists to sell us things and make us think we need more. I always remind myself that if the old masters of street photography were shooting on film cameras, capturing at best – if they were quick with their hands – a couple frames per second and with manual focus, then I've got no excuse with the capacity of the gear available today.

At the moment my primary camera is a Sony a7R IV. The drawback with this camera is that it's bigger and heavier than the Fuji cameras I've used in the past and the lenses are more expensive. I found my previous Fuji more ergonomic and easier to manipulate, but the image resolution is so high with the Sony that I can crop to enhance abstraction without sacrificing quality. I can do whatever I want with the image files, and they still look great. The lenses I use most regularly are 50mm and 85mm. This use came out of necessity. I live in Cambridge, UK, and almost always go out shooting around the city centre, which is a small area. If you shot with a wide-angle lens, so much of the background would enter into the frame, you'd only be able to shoot the same street so many times. Even if different things were happening, the photos would soon begin to look similar. With a long lens, you can isolate such a small portion of a scene that you could shoot on the same street for years, always producing different images.

Kit choice goes hand in hand with your approach to photography. The human drama-focused hunters, exemplified by Joel Meyerowitz, tend to use a wide-angle lens because they want as much going on as they can squeeze into the shot. Their style is defined by the lens, with their way of seeing the world channelled through their focal length. If you gave Bruce Gilden an 85mm or a 135mm lens, he wouldn't make the same work.

I always shoot in 'aperture priority'. Pretty much the only choice I make is how much I do or don't want to be in focus. Sometimes I'll do a more creative shot where I'll use a slower shutter speed, but beyond that, I'm really only concentrating on getting the composition right. I want to make as few decisions as possible. Is an image ISO 1600 or 3200? I don't care. No one is ever going to look at the image and say, it would have been good if it wasn't that tiny bit grainy because the ISO was whatever it was. But is the focus in the place where I meant it to be? Is the action frozen and the composition how I wanted it? Those are the things that matter when I consider if an image has been successful.

Occasionally, it's good to shake things up by giving yourself new restrictions when it comes to focal length or a camera type you're completely unfamiliar with. This forces you to experiment. This explains why many street photographers stick to prime lenses – because the limitation of a fixed focal length makes you more imaginative. You have to use your legs, make choices, and it's more interesting. I've got a zoom lens on my camera right now, which I use at the longer end of its focal range, and I'm not taking anything else with me. But I will use a wide-angle lens from time to time. I've got to work harder if I want to simplify a scene, to get something nice and clean with that – and harder still with a plastic toy camera with rusty batteries bought for the bargain price of £30.

'It's good to shake things up by giving yourself new restrictions when it comes to focal length or a camera type you're completely unfamiliar with.'

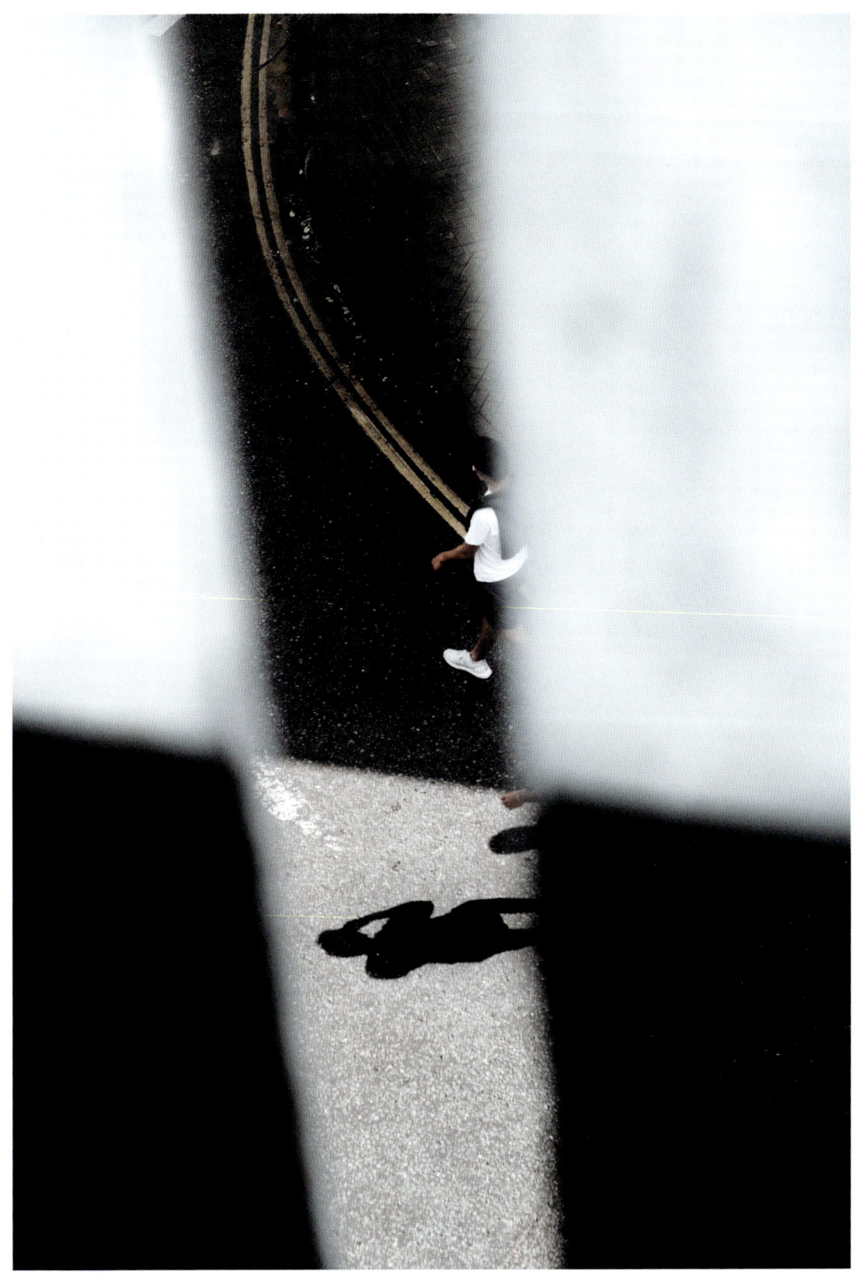

Restricting technical choices frees me up creatively to find striking compositions like this.
Cambridge, 2017

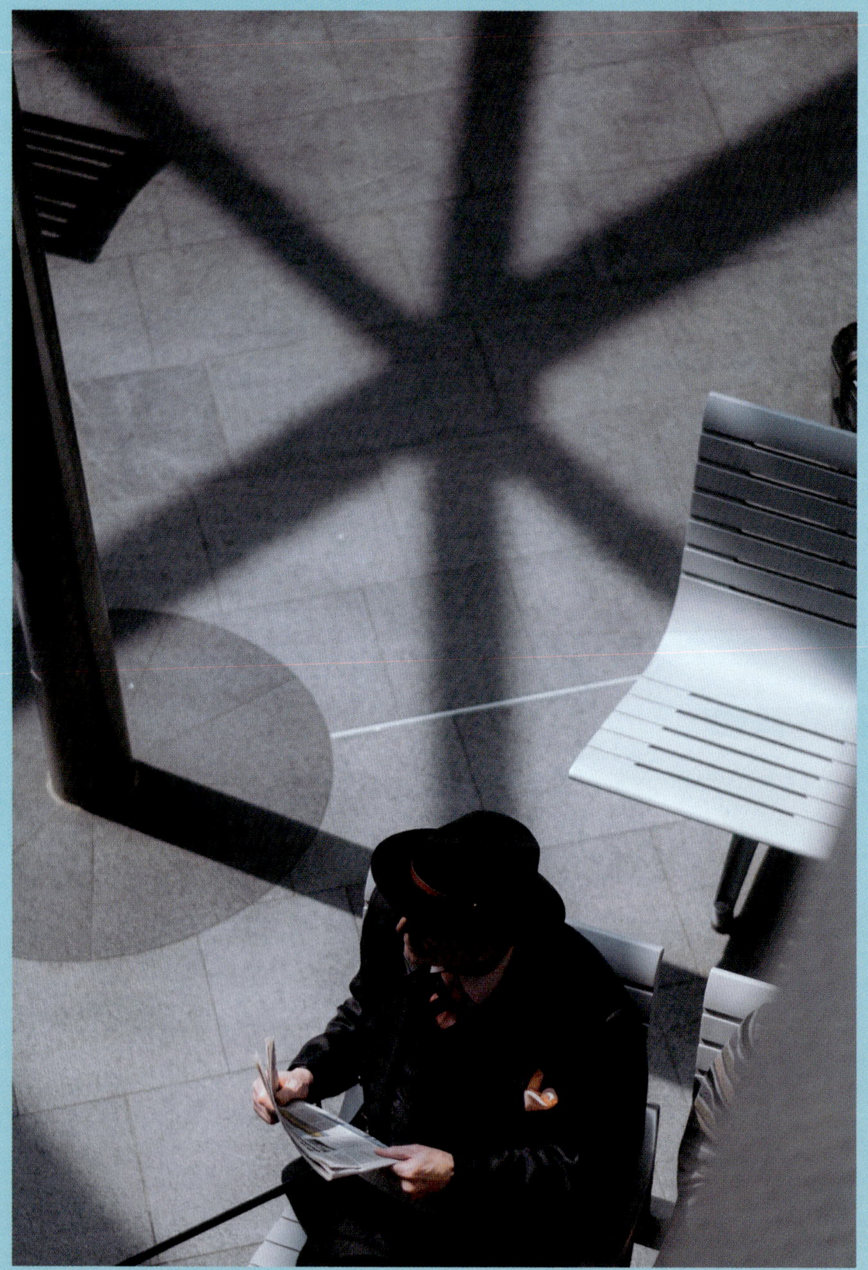

Little details – like this man's hat, handkerchief and tie – say a lot about someone.
London, 2018

4

Get out there

Think about when and where to go – but whatever you do, just go

In global megacities like London, New York, Tokyo or Delhi, you'll never be short of interesting things to photograph. When you're starting out, though, that can make things harder for you. Imagine being a trainee chef with every ingredient imaginable at your disposal – you wouldn't know what to do with them. But with just three ingredients, you're good to go. So, if you're lucky enough to be in a colossal city, you just have to deal with it by putting on your metaphorical blinkers and focusing on one element at a time, otherwise it is overwhelming. You might want to ease yourself in by focusing on just one aspect of a subject, as a way to tell the story of what they do.

Hands are great for this. Hands can give clues about what a person does in ways that their face won't necessarily reveal – paint stains that show they're an artist or the dusting of flour that suggests they're a baker. That tells you all you need to know. Faces, for me,

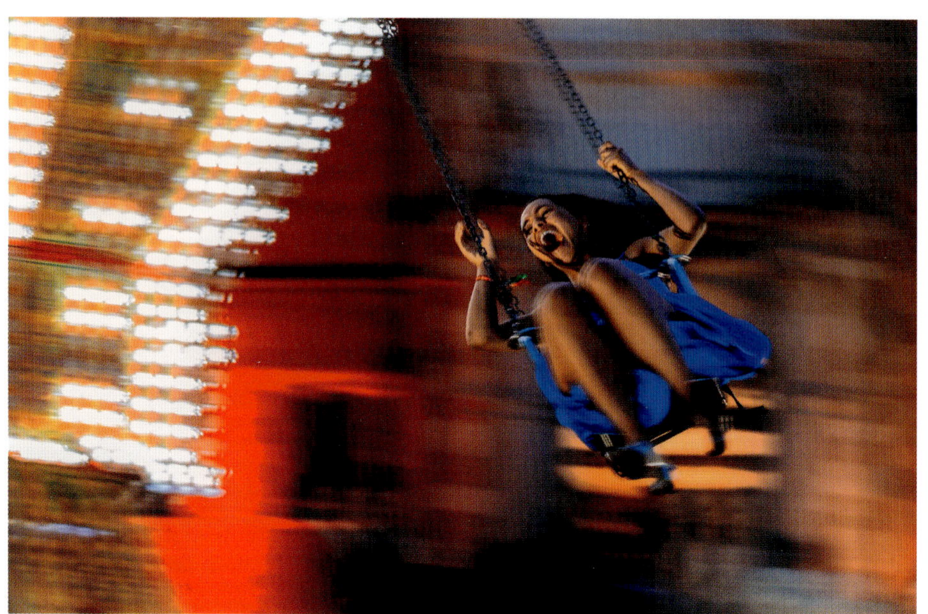

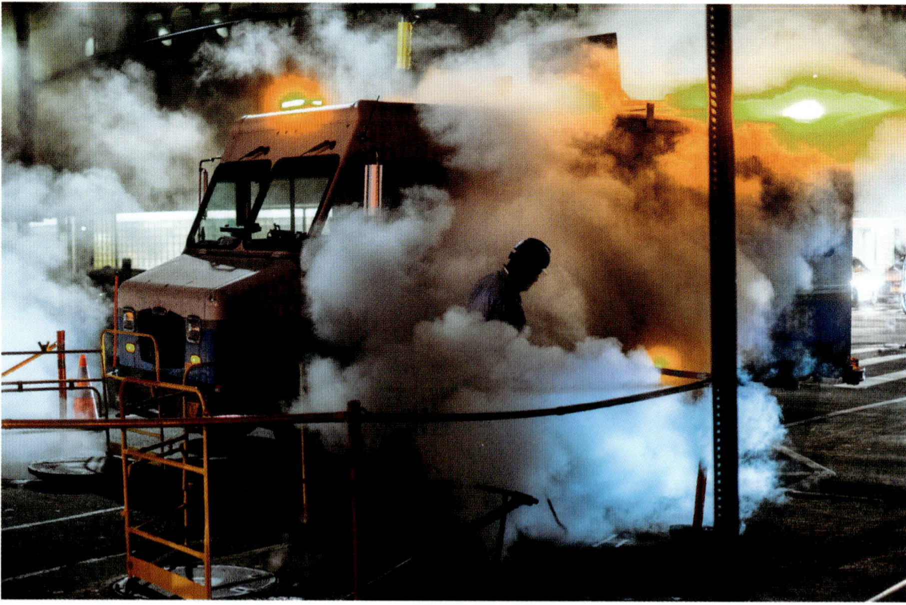

Motion blur and billowing steam give these shots a feeling of speed and texture.
ABOVE Cambridge, 2022
BELOW New York, 2018

are a distraction. What I want to portray is everything else besides. It's the light hitting a person. It's the movement of their clothes. It's the gesture they're making. It's the composition. As soon as there's a face there, psychologically, you're just hardwired to look straight at that. And then you miss the rest of it. I have a shot from 2017, of a guy wearing plastic gloves – what seemed strange at the time had become fairly commonplace by 2020, with the Covid-19 pandemic underway.

Breaking things down and setting yourself little tasks makes street photography a lot easier in the beginning. Then, once you've got to grips with that, you can just walk around looking at other things and observing the light to see how it changes throughout the day, or month by month, so that you can plan when to take the best picture. Apps such as PhotoPills can help with timing, as not everyone has the luxury of being able to check out the same spot at, say, 7am, then again at 9am, 10am, 11am and 12pm. For example, if you know a spot that would be great with the light coming in at a certain angle, you can use the app to look up the exact time of day and/or year that the light will be right. Then you can make a note of it and come back at the proposed time. Equally, head to locations where you can assume interesting things are likely to happen and research online to find out when there are public events that you can go to.

If I'm travelling to another city to shoot, I might check up on local events, but I won't have anything too specific in mind. When I'm in New York, shooting with the locals there, they might take me to unusual spots they know, but then, on the way, we often get sidetracked by something totally different. I was there in October of 2018, and I remember asking where I could see some steam coming out of pipes in the ground – it's a classic New York street shot. As we were heading to a place one of the guys knew, we bumped into a truck belonging to Con Edison, the company that maintains the city's electric, gas and steam network. And, right there, was a patch of ground they'd opened up, some 3m (10ft) wide and at least as deep, with a crazy chimney of steam rising up out of it. We just got really lucky there.

'Breaking things down and setting yourself little tasks makes street photography a lot easier in the beginning.'

I made my New York connections on Instagram. Before I went, I published a post saying that I was going to be there on those dates and asked who else wanted to shoot. Even if your followers are in the 1,000s, 100s even, you can still build up a network. A long time ago, when I had hardly any followers, I did a similar call out before a trip to Barcelona and someone got in touch telling me their cousin lived there. I sent them a DM and we met up. It's a really easy way to connect with people and find out about hidden food spots or other places that only insiders know. This cousin showed me the rooftop of his apartment block, which was really cool. It didn't lead to any shots, but it may well have and offered a way of seeing the city that wouldn't have been possible without that connection.

Being away somewhere and on a single-minded mission to shoot street photography is one thing, but if you don't have a week or so to spend taking pictures, but more like half an hour here and there, be sure to take it. The more time you spend out on the streets, the more you'll learn your craft and the more likely you are to get a good shot worth keeping. That's just maths. There is a direct relationship between how many hours you spend on the street and unique moments happening, but you can't engineer or predict when those moments will arise. They are the city's gift to you.

'The more time you spend out on the streets, the more you'll learn your craft and the more likely you are to get a good shot worth keeping.'

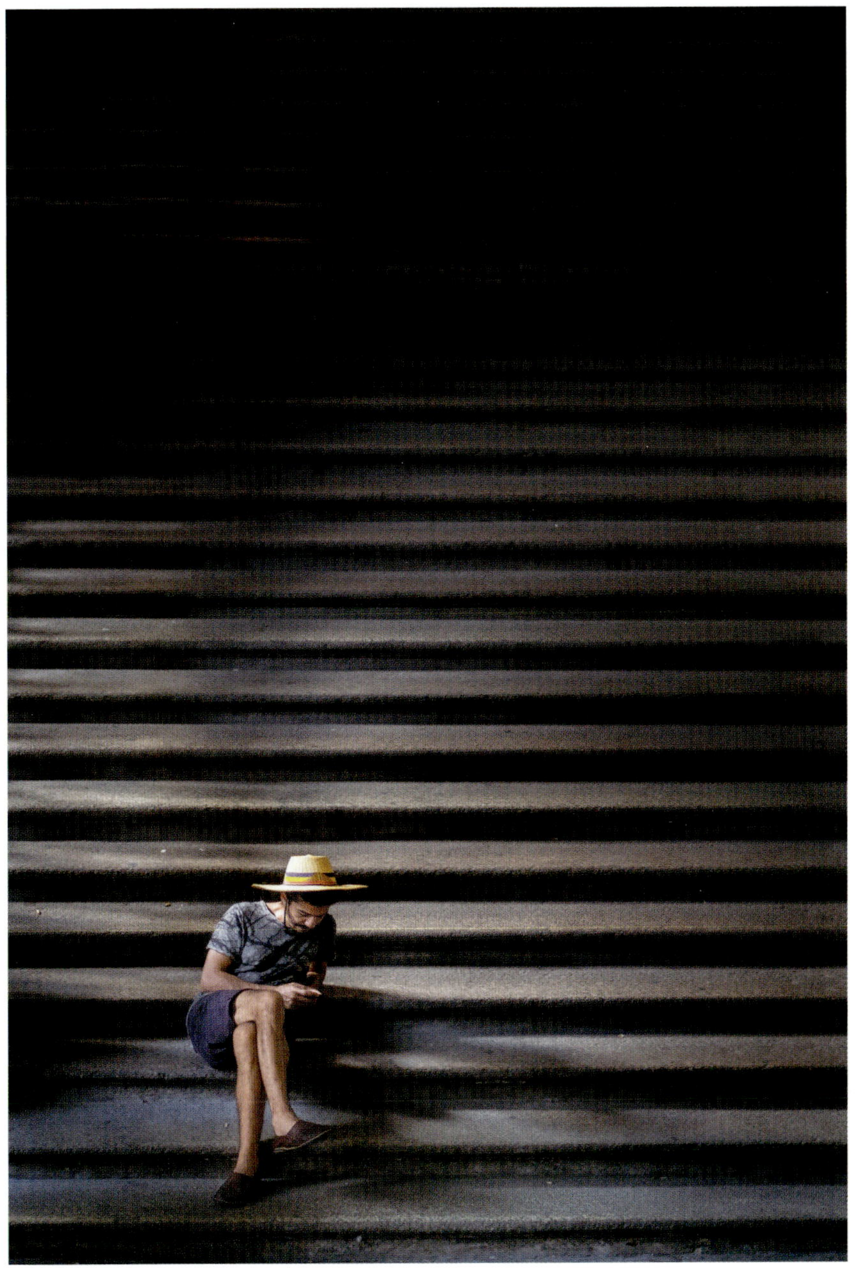

Find out from locals where to go for interesting backdrops, like these stone steps in Milan.
Milan, 2017

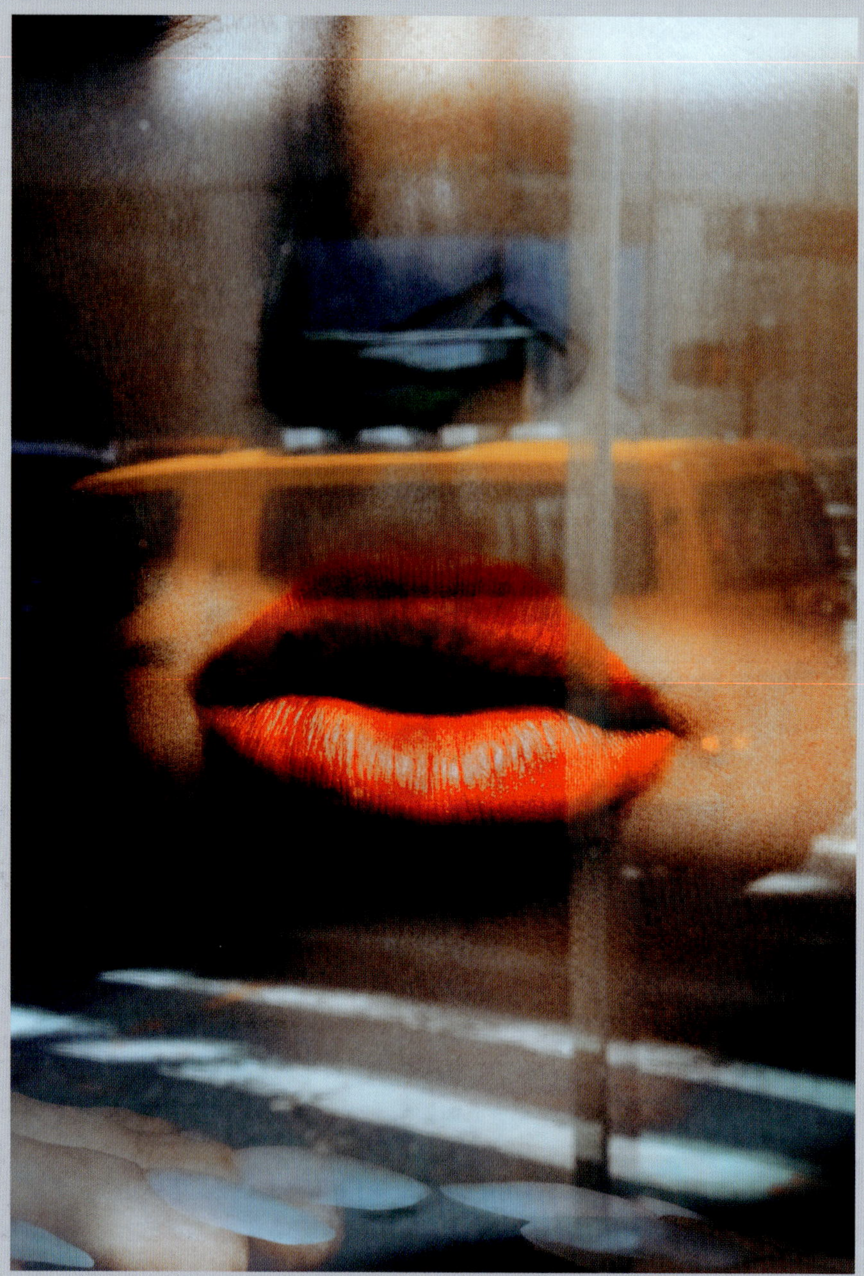

As soon as you get out, start taking pictures. And sometimes you'll strike gold.
New York, 2022

5

Limber up

To get the best street photography performance, do some warm-up exercises

The Canadian architect Frank Gehry doesn't know how to use a computer. The way he sparks ideas for his iconic designs is by free-form sketching. Sometimes, his pen takes him to a creative dead end; other times to places that no one would have predicted. His sketches are by no means accurate and to most people they look like scribbles, but when he's finished a project – the Guggenheim Museum Bilbao, say, or the Walt Disney Concert Hall in Los Angeles – he pulls out these random-looking jumbles of lines and the resemblance to the finished structure is uncanny.

Gehry's line drawings have dual benefits. On the one hand, they open him up to the possibility of happy accidents and this is probably how he came up with some of his best ideas. But they also avoid the blank canvas feeling that many creatives get. 'Blank canvas' might seem an odd reference for a photographer when the world is out there offering itself up to be recorded, but we can

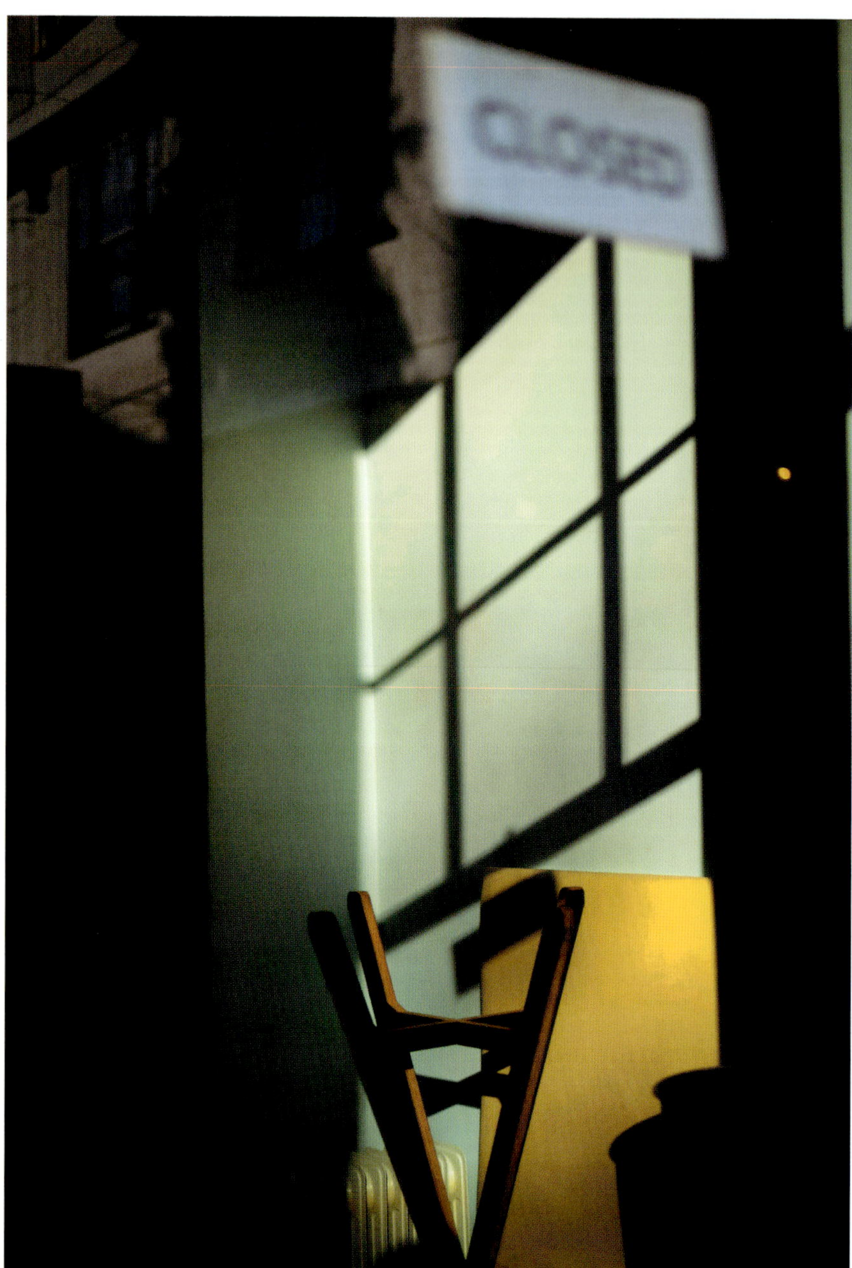

The more pictures you take, the more attuned your eye will become to spot moments like this.
Cambridge, 2018

undergo something similar. Luckily, we're living in the digital age, so we can take thousands of pictures at relatively little cost compared to buying and processing rolls and rolls of film. And what might have taken photographers 50 years of experimenting with different light situations to perfect, should be much quicker for us to get to grips with.

So, crack on. If you shoot a dud picture, it's no loss, you can just review it, delete it and retake it. This gives you the license to experiment and it also means that, when you're out on the streets, you can warm up by taking test shots, and plenty of them. Think of yourself as a runner about to hit the track for the 100m final or an actor about to go on stage in the finale of a sold-out run. These test shots are your star jumps and stretches or your blocking and vocal exercises. I did the same thing when I was studying illustration – I'd just start making marks on paper. Sometimes it's good to set yourself a challenge. Like drawing with your non-dominant hand, you could start shooting with your aperture wide open. This all helps your brain to get into the right mode to take great pictures – it would be foolish to go straight into it.

There's a noble history of street photographers doing exactly this. American photographer Garry Winogrand used to walk out and just compulsively start hitting the shutter on his camera, literally taking photos of everything indiscriminately. Over the course of his life, according to a US documentary about his work called *All Things are Photographable*, it's estimated that he took more than a million pictures. Luckily, now, we're not just burning through film when we try to do the same.

Personally, I take fewer photos now than I used to when I was first starting out. It's partly knowing my city well and partly that I've got pickier. There are times when I just walk around for an hour without taking any photographs. On other days, I'll take photographs that look like nothing – empty frames, devoid of any human activity and of little interest whatsoever to anyone. I don't care, because these test shots are exactly that – tests. I see them as disposable and that frees me up not to worry about getting something remarkable. Paradoxically, some of my favourite images have come about this way.

'If you shoot a dud picture, it's no loss, you can just review it, delete it and retake it.'

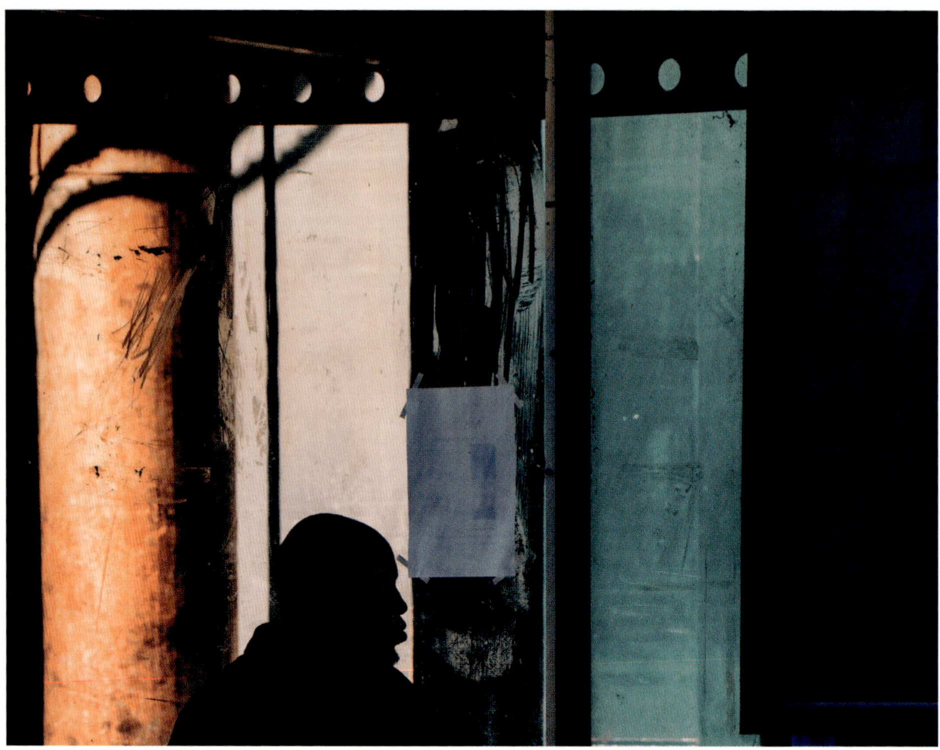

This is a perfect alignment of alternating columns of colour, topped off with a silhouette profile.
Cambridge, 2022

As you start to improve, you'll raise your standards and that will make you more discerning. Now, I can almost do in my head what the camera would be doing. I'm constantly observing what is around me and building up compositions in my mind. If I'm walking around a scene that I've seen many times, on a street I go down every day, it can be hard to lift a camera to shoot something unless it is completely out of the ordinary. My standards have been raised so high that if something's not spectacular, I don't even shoot it. Take it from me that this is a terrible habit and one that goes against my own advice! I sometimes need to remind myself to loosen up and keep experimenting. But I think that happens to everyone – whether you're a street photographer or an actor or an architect. You always want to keep pushing yourself to make better work than you've made in the past.

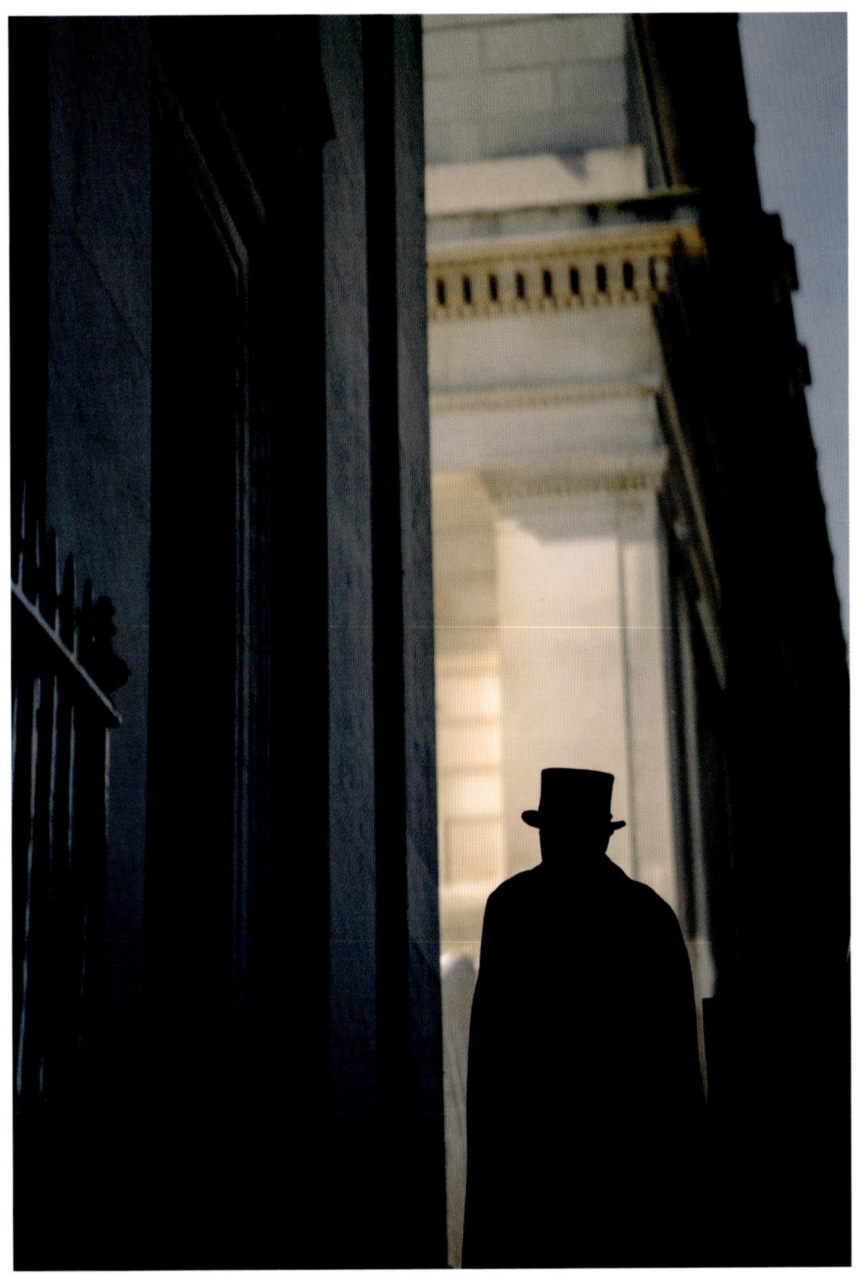

The intersection of these buildings set the stage for the right figure to come along.
Cambridge, 2022

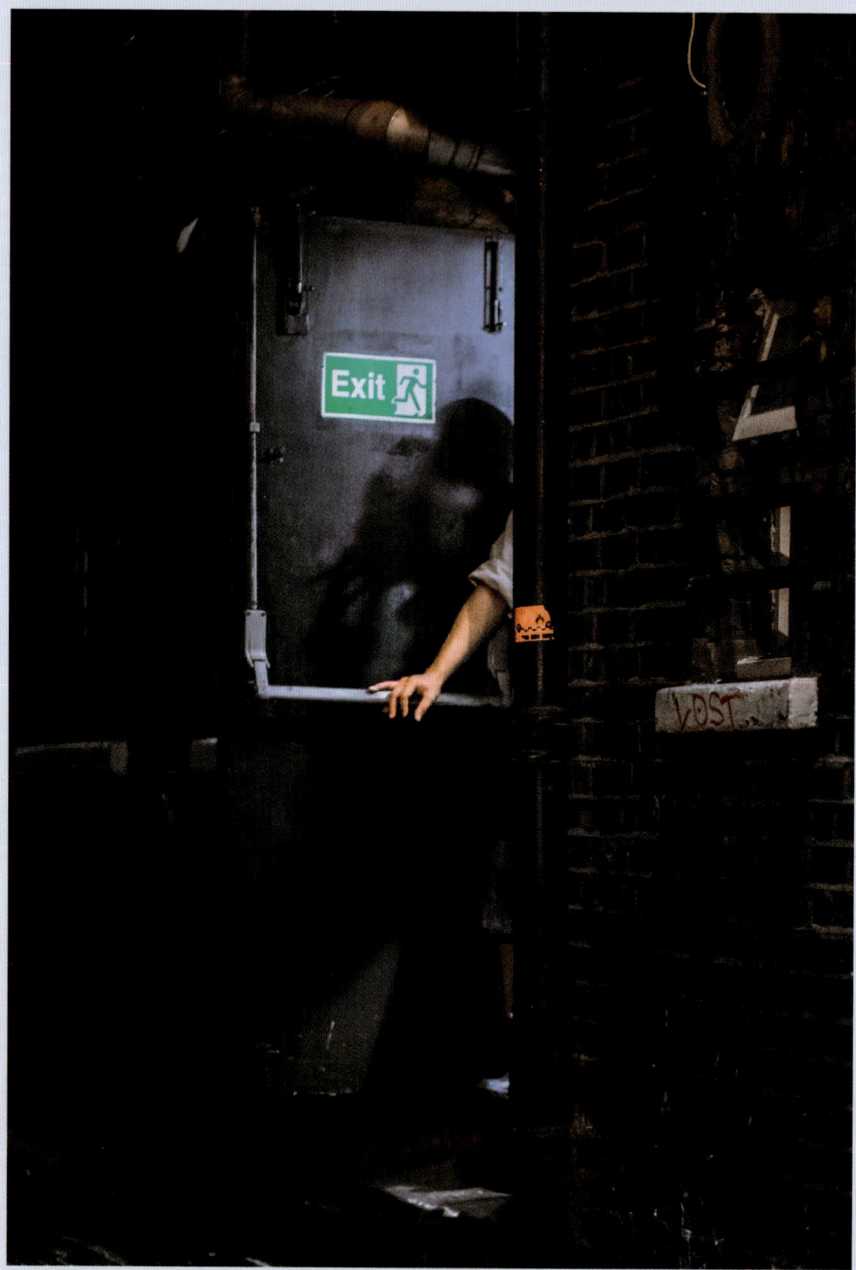

Looking at this shot, we don't know whether the door is opening or closing – we're intrigued.
London, 2017

6

Scope the scene

**Close observation tells you
what's about to go down,
so you're ready when it does**

If a door is slightly ajar, something is almost certainly about to happen. At any moment, a person will walk in or out. Perhaps as they do, they'll push the door wide open so you get a sudden flash of what's going on inside. When you hit the streets with your camera, this is exactly the kind of scenario you need to look out for – cues that tell you what might be about to unfold. When you're warming up, taking random shots, you're looking, listening, imbibing absolutely everything in the street – the noises, the lights, the traffic, the conversations. The gaggles of tourists, the pigeons, the changing digital advertising and, of course, the open doors – they're all perfect frames within a frame just waiting for the subject to arrive.

The more time you spend observing, the better. For me, this has become instinctive, and I can never completely switch off. I'm looking at the light, looking at shapes and reflections, weighing up how they could form into compositions. It comes from having trained

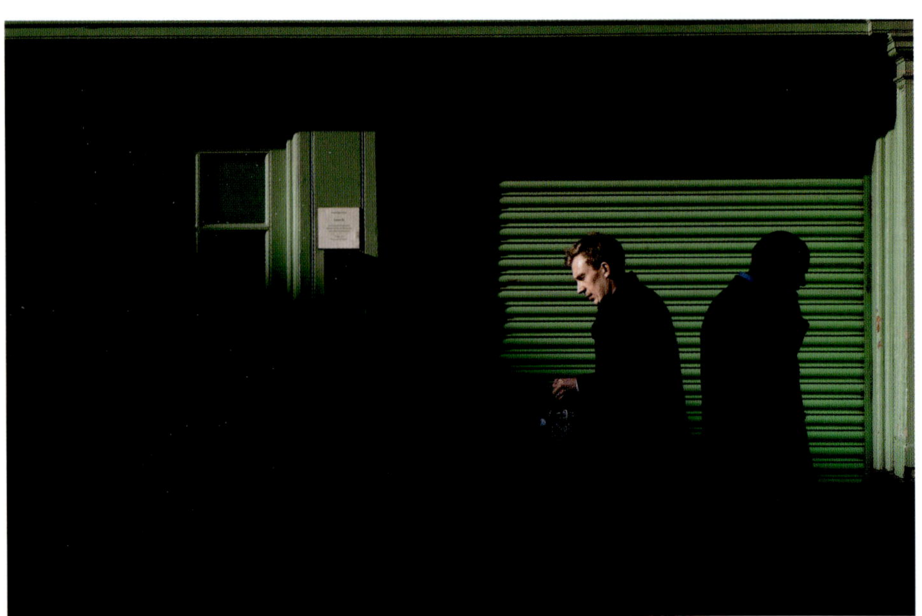

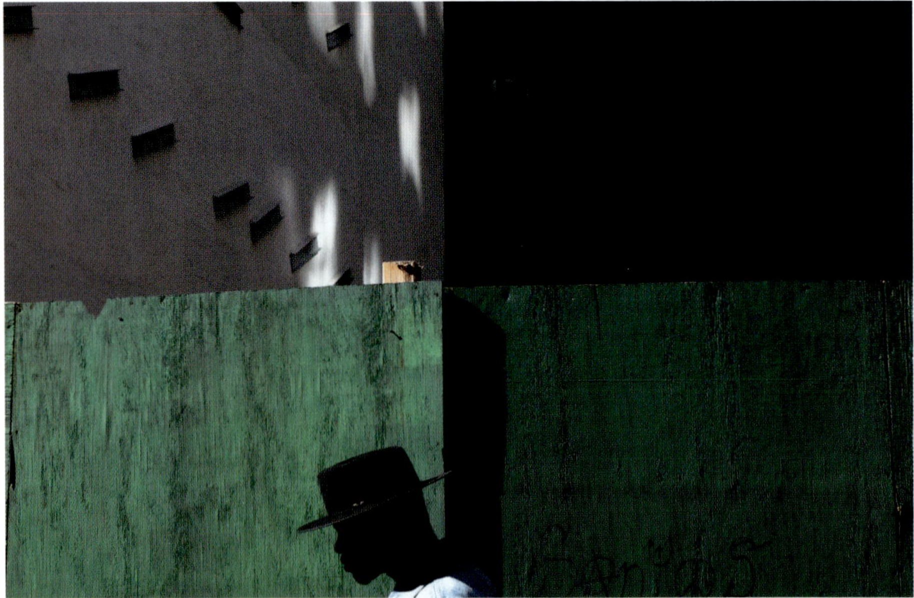

Achieve a graphic look by using block-colour backgrounds, like these shutters and boards.
ABOVE London, 2018
BELOW New York, 2018

my eye over years to view the world from every imaginable angle. When you're scoping things out, try putting your hand over one eye, preferably the dominant one. You might get some funny looks but ignore them. By limiting what you see, you start to pick up on things that you might otherwise miss. For me, it helps flatten out depth so I can focus on how layers of foreground, midground and background line up. There are always at least 10 ways to approach a shot – try this from a range of angles and eventually you'll strike gold.

'When you're warming up, taking random shots, you're looking, listening, imbibing absolutely everything in the street.'

When I'm out in my hometown, Cambridge, I'm always on the alert for what's new and if it's a transient feature of the street, so much the better. The pace of urban change is phenomenal. Even if you're in the same town centre from one day to the next, certain aspects could look unrecognisable. On one road, there might be a shop that's gone out of business and is being redeveloped so the shopfront is boarded up while there's building work being carried out. Temporarily, that gives you a handy, solid white background to use for silhouettes. When it comes to the crowds, the questions I ask myself are things like: What are people wearing? Where are they standing? What are they doing? What are they holding? Their clothes, positions and props are all compositional elements I can incorporate into shots.

In the beginning as a street photographer, you can feel as if you're constantly playing catch up with the city. You see a striking figure, raise the camera, take the shot and … 99 times out of 100 it's going to result in the least captivating version of a picture of that person. But if you walk around first, scoping out the scene, you can bank potential compositions to keep up your sleeve – you've got a frame in mind with a vivid red area, a place where there's good light or a nice shape in a window. Then, when the perfect subject happens to be passing, you know which elements you can work with. So, don't be lazy, don't take the shot straight away. Run up the street, be primed with your composition and wait for your subject to come along or, as you get more confident, you can follow behind them and compose with the element you had in mind.

Working in pairs is another great way to approach things when you're starting out, especially if you're timid. Four eyes can be better than two! You can share observations and it's interesting to

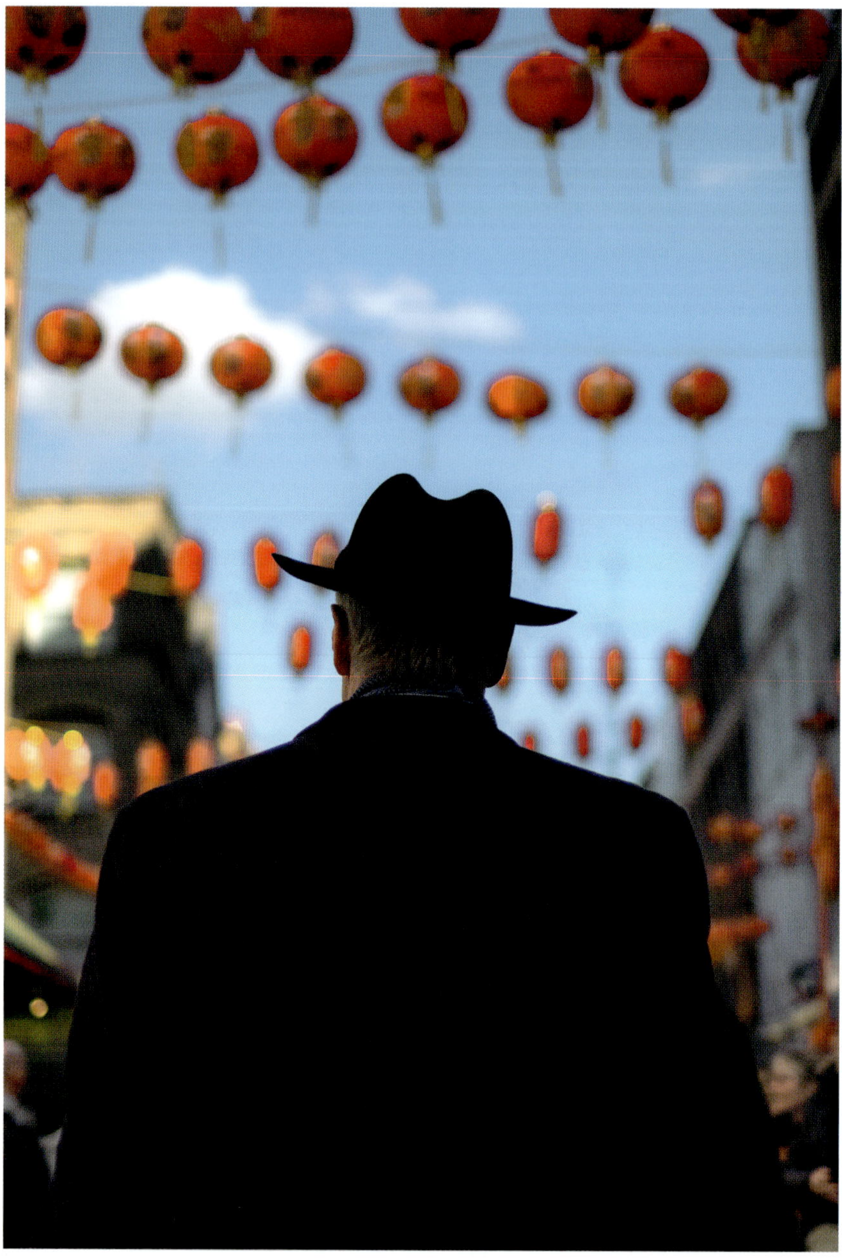

    Find Your Frame

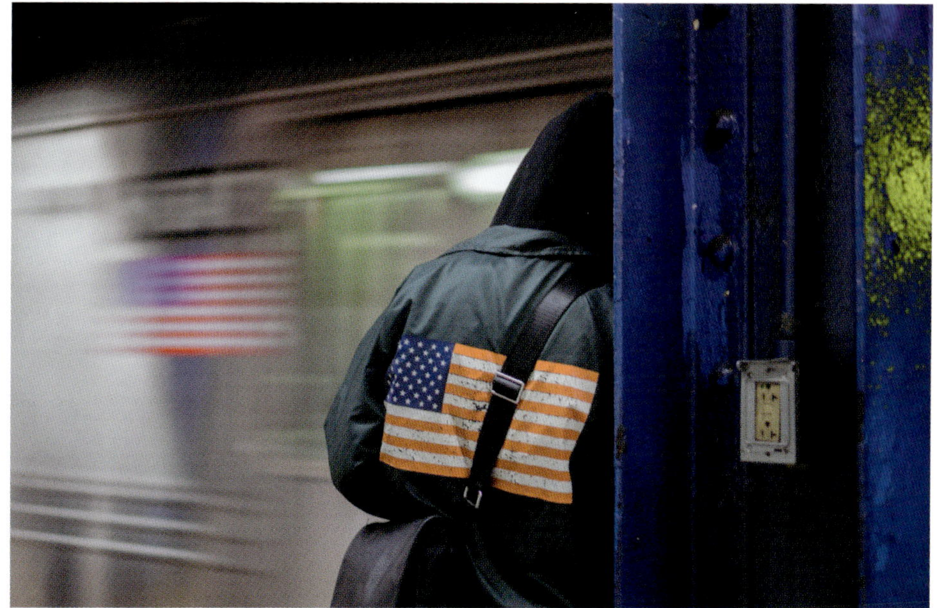

see how the images you come back with reflect your subjective ways of seeing the world, even if you're photographing the same location. Working alone, you risk getting tunnel vision about something but when you're with someone else, they can point you in the direction of other shots and offer you a challenge as well. Maybe they spot something first and jump straight on to the most obvious composition – if you really want a shot of that too, you're going to have to think harder and find your own way of interpreting it.

Occasionally, when you've scoped out a scene, your moment doesn't arrive until days later. On one of my New York trips, there was a guy standing in front of me on a subway platform. The train came to a stop and I shot a few frames with a slow shutter speed just to capture the blurred train beyond him. And then, a couple of days later, I was back on the subway platform and a girl walked in front of me wearing a bomber jacket emblazoned with the Stars and Stripes. I remembered that when I'd taken the shot of the other guy, I'd noticed that every single subway carriage is painted with the American flag. Instantly, I realised I should photograph this girl with the train going by at the same slow shutter speed. I knew there and then that I'd nailed the better shot.

If you've done the groundwork, when the right person comes along, you'll know it.

LEFT
London, 2018

ABOVE
New York, 2018

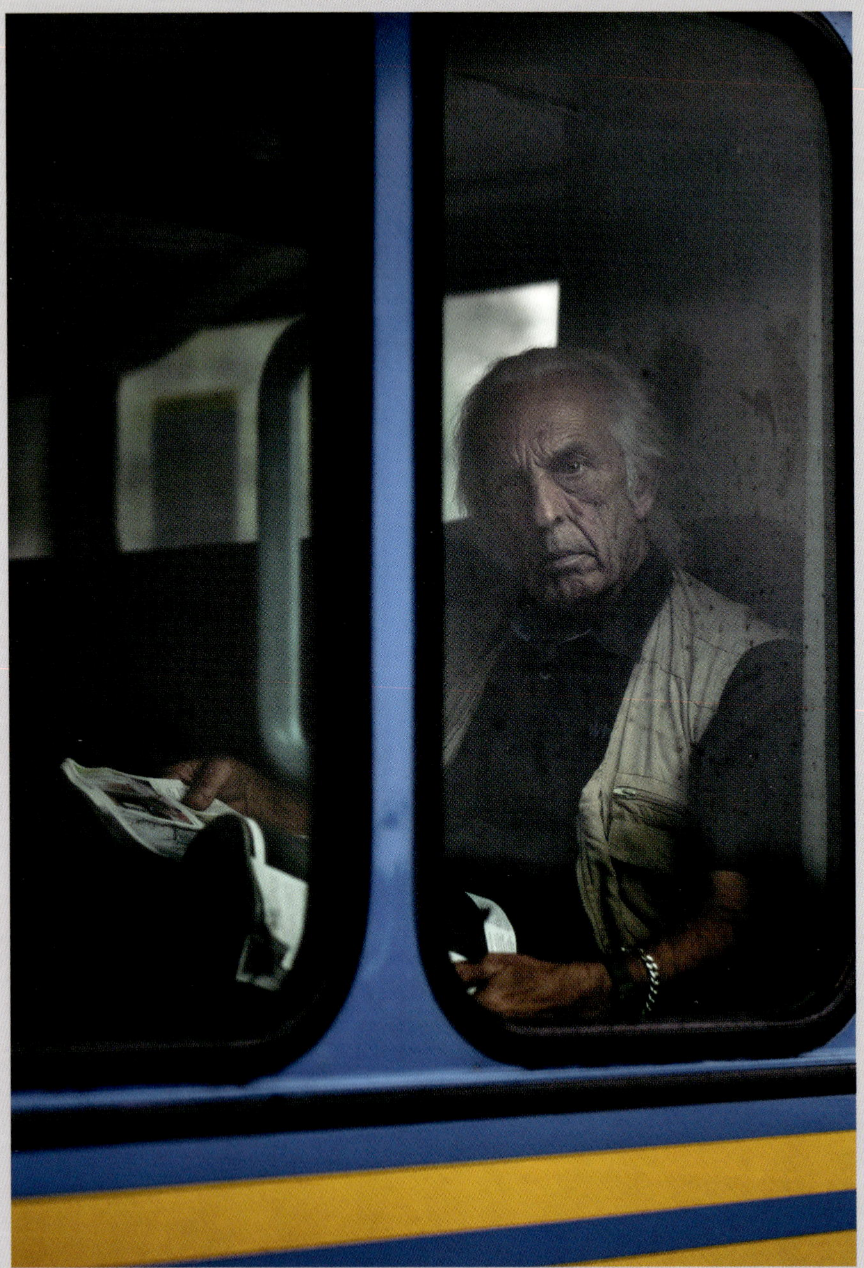

You can't quite tell here if the subject is looking at you or not. There's a sense of mystery to it.
Cambridge, 2017

7

Don't be shy

Be confident and leave your inhibitions at home, they'll only hold you back

There's a feeling you sometimes have when you're about to take a picture. Your stomach drops and you get a surge of adrenaline, a fight-or-flight response. You might experience it as a social anxiety. Your mind might start racing, firing off questions… What will that person think of me? How do I get myself into the right position without attracting attention? Is this a good idea? That is your brain telling you that you're looking at something compelling, something you must photograph. It's your cue to run forward and hit the shutter.

Whenever I do workshops, beginners always ask me how to deal with that awkwardness? Everybody goes through it at the start, but you must get past it. Anyone who's been shooting on the street for a while will have faced a moment like this. If they've pushed through, they will have come out the other side a different photographer. Even if you don't and then go on to specialise in

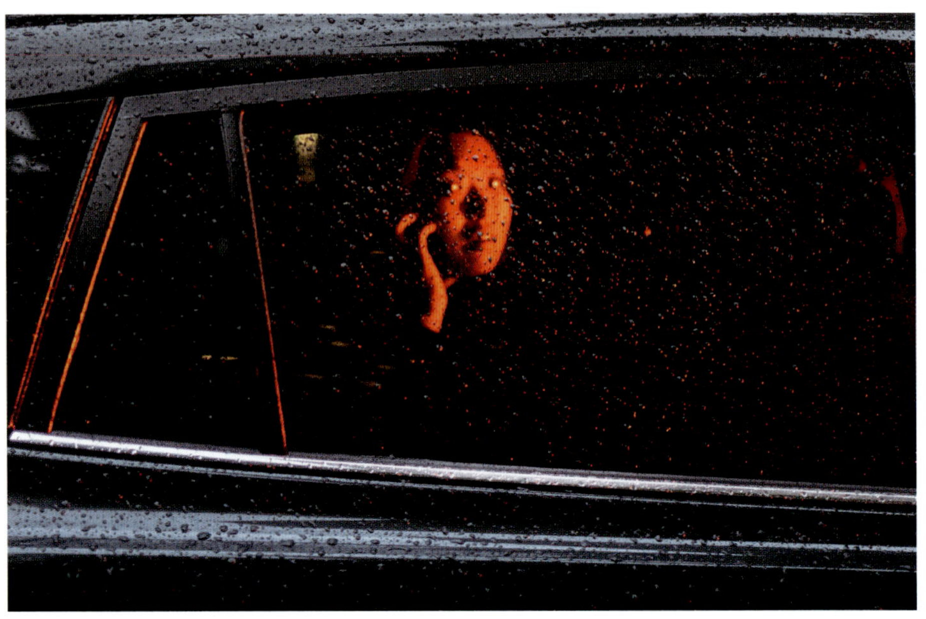

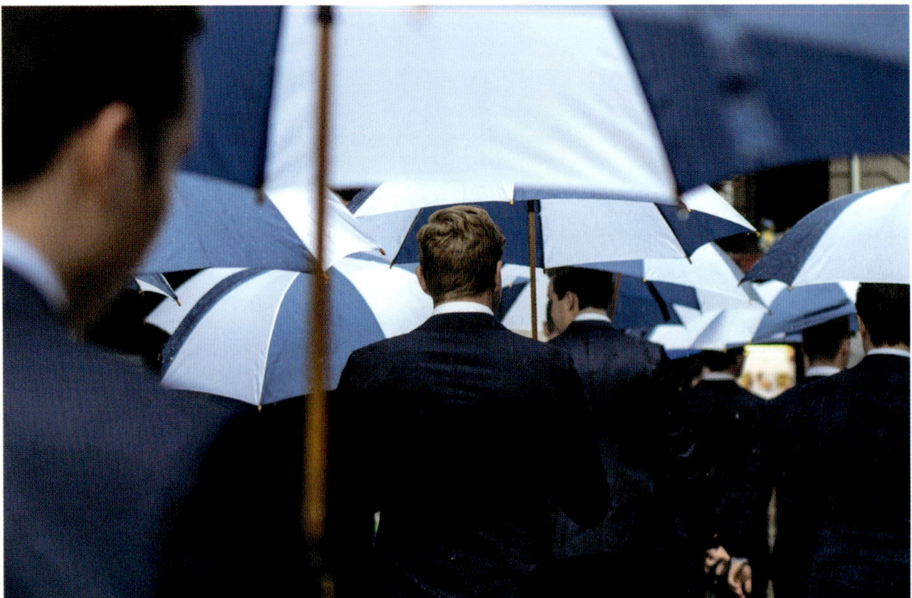

Stand proud. If you're self-assured, people don't question or even notice what you're doing.
ABOVE New York, 2019
BELOW New York, 2019

photographing people, you know that in 10 years' time if you see
a rare and interesting scene involving a person or some people that
you absolutely must capture, you're not going to miss it out of shyness.
Because you've made that leap already.

I remember my awkward moment. There was a bus driver
staring daggers at me, straight into the lens. I was on my bike, on my
way home from work, when I rode past him. I braked, jumped off
and headed back. I'd made this agreement with myself earlier that
if I pulled the brakes for even a split second thinking this might be a good shot, I had to stop. Otherwise, I knew I'd find myself stewing with regret. This was the first time I followed through on that. At the time, it's like there are two parts of you battling it out – the photographer, who just wants the shot, and the human thinking, 'This is going to be weird, uncomfortable or dangerous.' If taking a shot is dangerous, you must listen to that instinct, but if it's just uncomfortable, you have to get over it.

It could be, as in my case with the bus driver, a situation where
you feel some hostility or it could just be tricky engineering yourself
into the right spot to get the composition you want. For some
pictures to work, you want the person to look directly into the lens,
so you need to step forward and get their attention to make that
happen. Know that the shot is worth more than a stranger's opinion
of you. They might just think, 'Oh, that guy was weird. Who cares?'
In seven years of doing this, I've only ever encountered one person
who was angry. I've only been asked to delete a picture on two
occasions, and both times it was all very polite.

You need to understand the effect of your body language.
Avoid looking casual or lazy – like having one hand in your pocket,
for example. If you act as if you're doing something wrong, people
will respond to you as though that's the case. A simple smile goes
a long way – I've got a shot from New York where the entire frame
is filled with guys in suits holding umbrellas. But there were two
people with them who weren't in suits and I didn't want to include
them in the picture because they'd detract from it. To get the shot,
I positioned myself between them and the suits. I turned round,
caught their eyes and smiled. They saw that it was an interesting
scene, too, and when I was done, they even asked me for a copy.

'If you act as if you're doing something wrong, people will respond to you as though that's the case.'

If there's a stag do or similar going on, you'll often find that one person in the group sees you taking the photo – but they're in on the joke. They're willing you on, thinking, 'I want there to be a photo of this because it's funny.' And then you can get right into the frame. It's about observing, interpreting any given situation and playing off that. But you can use all sorts of tricks. Occasionally, someone will spot that I've made eye contact with them accidentally while I'm getting an idea of what my composition is going to be and I don't want them to be looking into the lens. But if I pick up the camera at that moment, that's exactly what's going to happen. So, I try to go incognito. I might walk past them, wait a few seconds and then double back on myself to quickly get the shot or I might get my phone out and hang there for long enough that I've melted into the background, almost becoming part of the street furniture. Once they forget you're even there, you can take the shot and then off you go.

You can switch up the power dynamics, too. Say you frame up something so you've got your composition ready, and you're waiting for someone to walk through to complete the shot. In this situation, people are aware of what you are doing and if they walk through, that's their choice, so you can take as many shots as you want. But in some places, like the UK, people are inherently polite. You might be waiting for a subject to walk through your composition, but they see you with your camera, and stop, wary that they're going to ruin the shot. In situations like this, I tend to drop the camera and give them a friendly grin to reassure them it's okay for them to walk on. Then, the second they get level with me, I lift up the camera again and take the shot. That's the easiest one when you're starting out – framing up first and letting people walk through. There's no risk there at all because it's obvious what you're doing.

Getting more confident on the street comes from spending time there. You don't even need to have a camera with you. You can just walk around, watching the world. Athletes and gamers talk about being 'in the zone' and this is not so different. There's a point at which you spend enough time in a space that you start understanding what's about to happen and you can subconsciously pre-empt it. Eventually, you just get a gut feeling that makes you lift the camera at the right time and it all flows together.

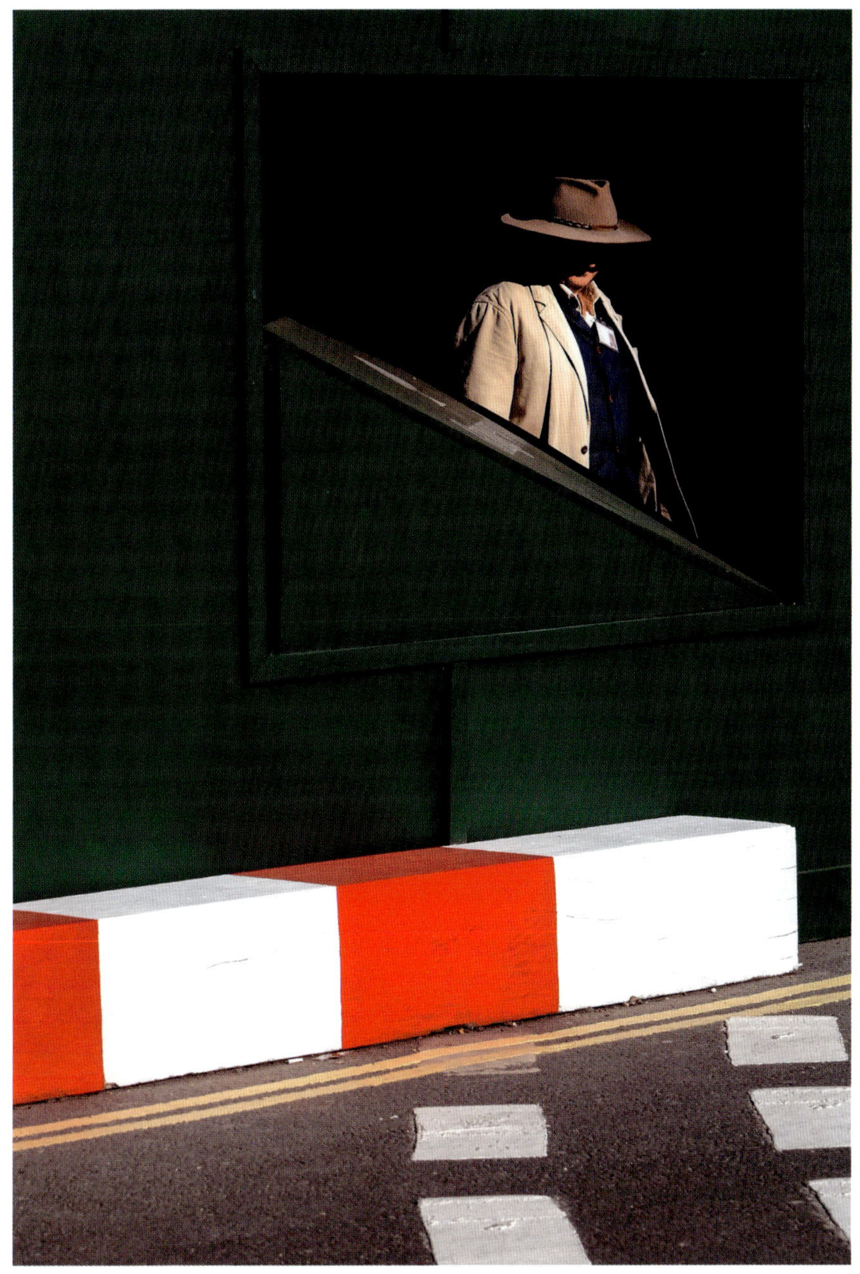

After a while, you don't give people much thought. You and they are simply part of the scene.
London, 2017

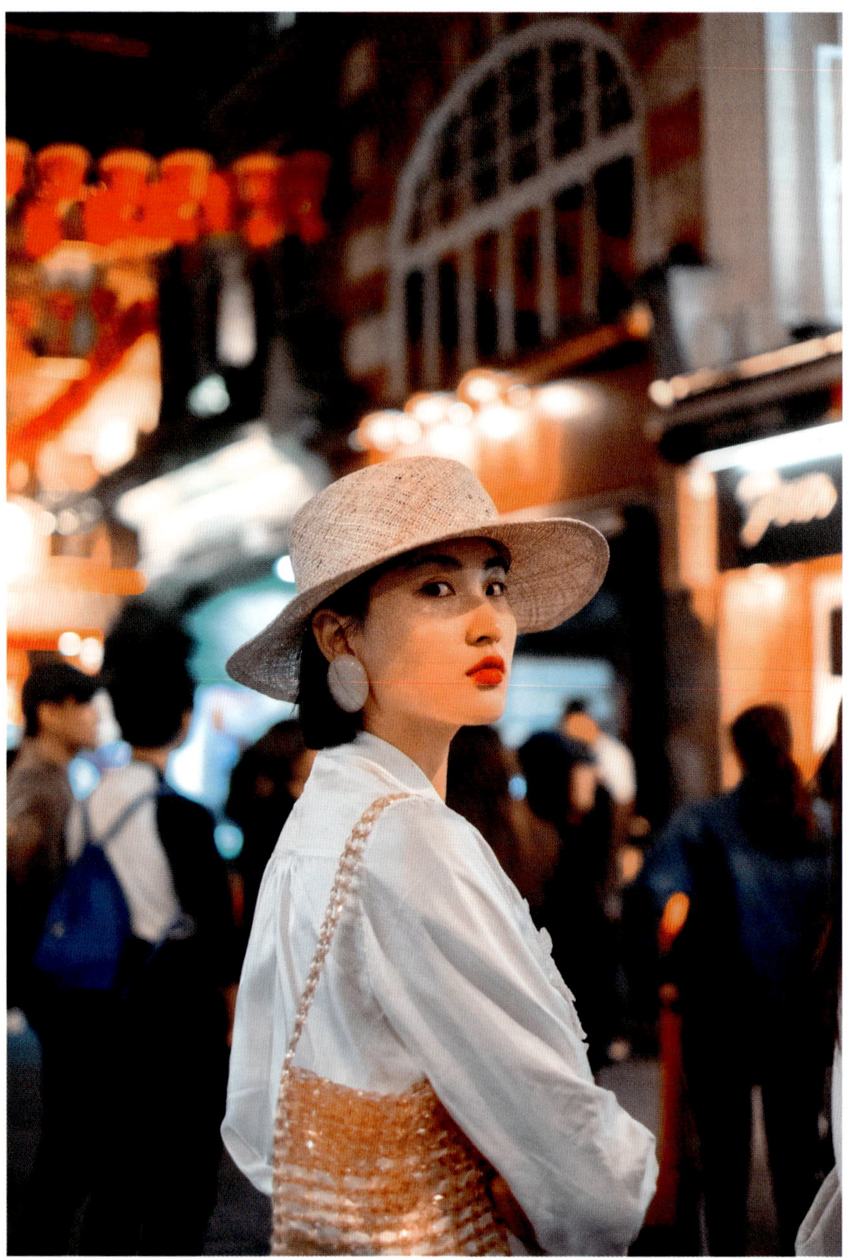

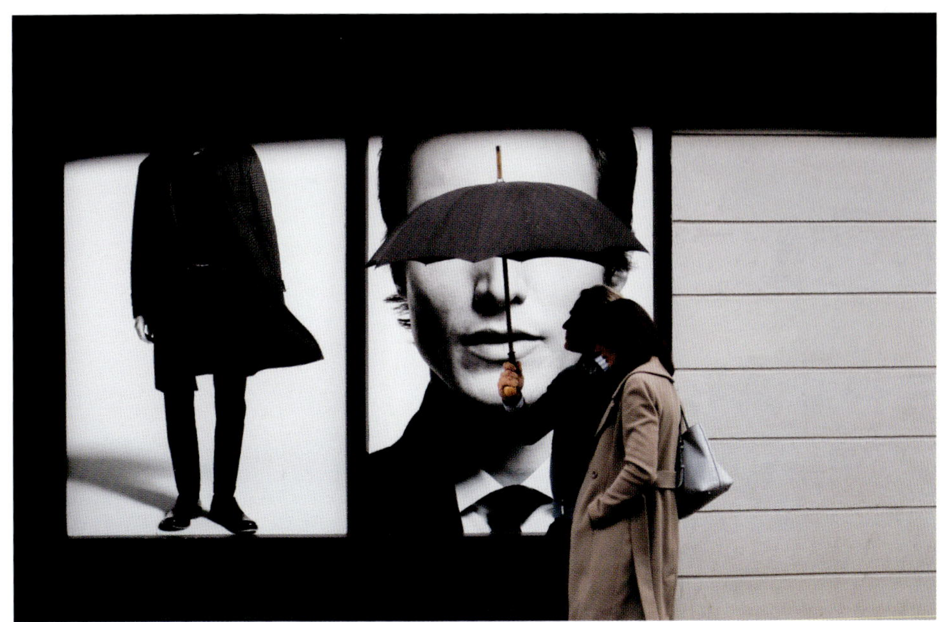

'If taking a shot
is dangerous, you
must listen to that
instinct, but if it's just
uncomfortable, you
have to get over it.'

Sometimes embracing
social tension is the
making of a shot;
other times it's best
to blend in.

LEFT
London, 2018

ABOVE
Cambridge, 2018

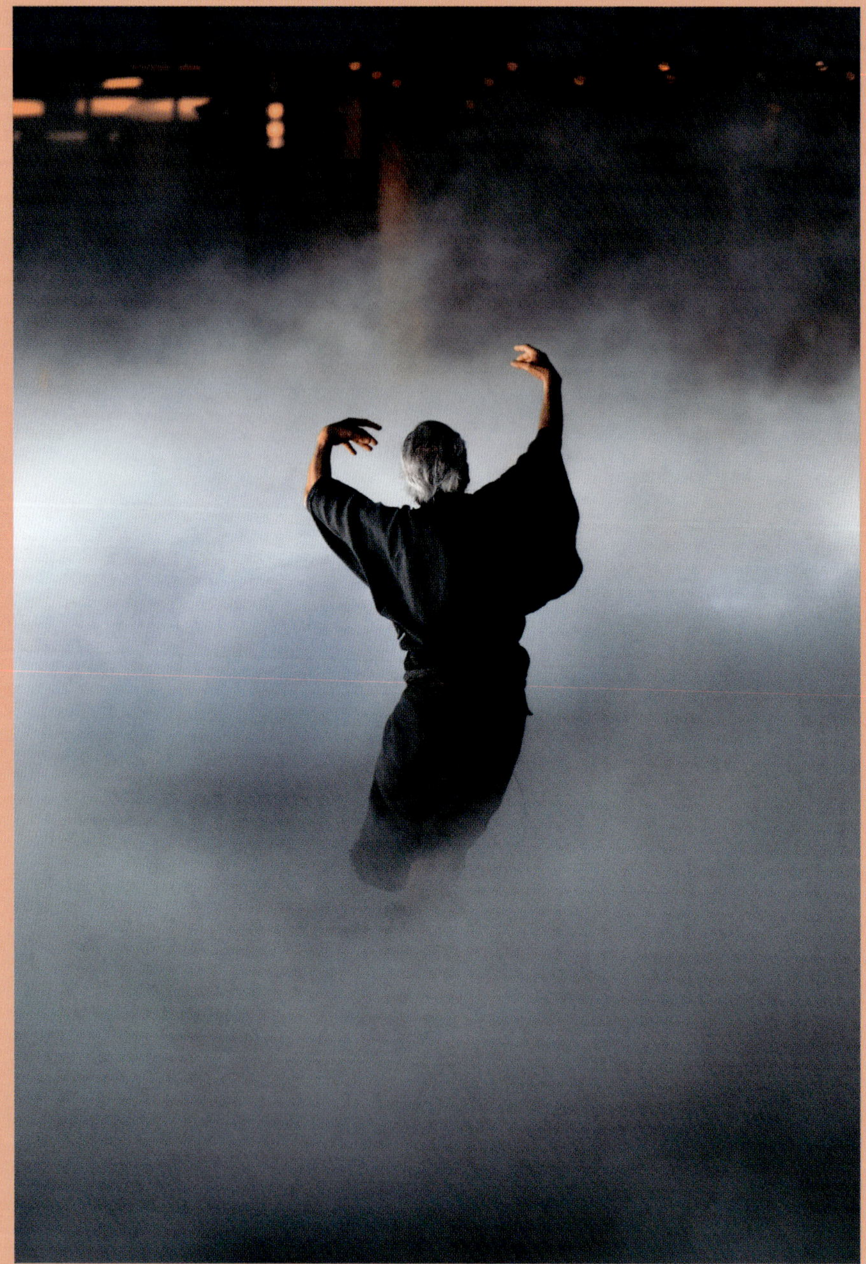

The drama in this shot would be lost if I'd hit the shutter a split second before or after.
London, 2017

8

Spot one-offs

Keep your eyes peeled for unreproducible occurrences, whether human or otherwise

In 1967, a man tripped over and fell on a Parisian pavement, landing flat on his back. Legendary American street photographer Joel Meyerowitz was right there, Leica in hand, to capture the immediate aftermath – a cyclist turning back amid the traffic to see what had happened, a workman stepping gingerly over the man as he lay in the street. More than five decades on, the New Yorker looks back on this as one of the photographs that makes him most proud. It's a scene where not much is happening and yet everything is happening – the drama of life crystallised by the varying reactions of different passers-by offers an insight into how humans relate to one another – or not – when they live, as many of us do, in a big city.

Fallen Man, as the shot is known, is exactly the kind of random instance that people picture when they think of street photography. In some ways, it's a very different approach to mine. Instead of hunting for these mini urban dramas, I tend to build up compositions

I hit the jackpot when this man looked up from under his umbrella as the ambulance passed.
New York, 2019

creatively using colour, shape and geometry, including human figures to finish off the shot. Randomness does play a role in my work, though. Sometimes I'll have a strong composition preformed and then, by luck, someone or something completely unique comes along. But, equally, being in the habit of preemptively building those compositions makes me much faster at reacting to a unique moment when I see it – say, in cases where I spot an event unfolding from afar and have to run to capture the shot. Either way, I don't hang around. I don't usually wait more than half an hour – I'd rather just come back another day.

'Ask yourself what possibilities you have for composition at that precise time.'

There's a picture that I made on a trip to New York that is a good example of how I work with chance. I was standing on the street as an ambulance came by. The ambulance stopped, I took some shots of a girl in a car with the ambulance's red light shining through the window. I thought, 'That's that,' and wandered on until I saw this guy standing under an umbrella by the entrance to the NBC building. I wondered, what can I compose with this? Just then, the ambulance took off again. By that point, I had the composition ready, I didn't even need to look! I could hear the siren, I knew what was going to happen. But my intention was also obvious to the man outside the NBC building and he kept dropping his umbrella so it covered his face. Every now and then he'd lift it up to check if I was still pointing the camera at him and, just one of those times, the flashing red light hit his face and everything came together perfectly. I was probably there for 30 seconds, but it was enough.

Another is a photograph of a woman in a niqab so that only her eyes are showing, who happens to be standing right by an advertisement that has been torn to reveal another pair of eyes. I was in London, out shooting with another photographer, when I took this. Like the previous example, it's a combination of setting things up, putting myself in the right place and then the unpredictable process of waiting for a person to complete the shot. In fact, there was a slightly stronger composition to have had here, but there was just no way to get it at the time because of the position we were in. If we had been further back, we could also have included some text on the ad which read 'watch this space'. The other photographer came back the next day and waited for three and a half hours to get a shot with that in the frame and another woman in a niqab staring straight down the lens.

In the early days, when something cool happens and you don't get the shot, you might kick yourself for missing it. Maybe you didn't have the camera in your hands, or switched on, or you weren't quick enough off the mark. It can be gutting. But the chances are, three seconds later the person will do exactly the same thing. People repeat behaviours all the time. It's always worth lifting the camera again on the off-chance. I remember missing a shot of a couple kissing on the London Underground. When they kissed, their faces disappeared behind one of the poles for passengers to hold on to. I thought they wouldn't do that again, but picked up my camera anyway, and they did! There have been other times when I've found a glass door to shoot through, waited patiently for something to appear on the other side and when, finally, someone puts their hand on it, they take it away – only to put it back seconds later, making my frustration thankfully short-lived.

More often than not, the random factor in an image of mine does not come down to people. It could relate to a light source or some animated signage. What counts is that it's something that will never occur again in exactly the same way – there is no chance that another photographer could come along and reproduce the same shot. It's about originality. I've sat there, poised, waiting for the moment it changes. But not all random moments make great pictures. You have to ask yourself what possibilities you have for composition at that precise time. There might be someone doing something interesting, but the background behind them is messy. The moment simply won't stand out. No matter how unusual the scene unfolding in front of you, that alone won't cut it. The shot has to be well composed. Always ask yourself what potential compositions you have available.

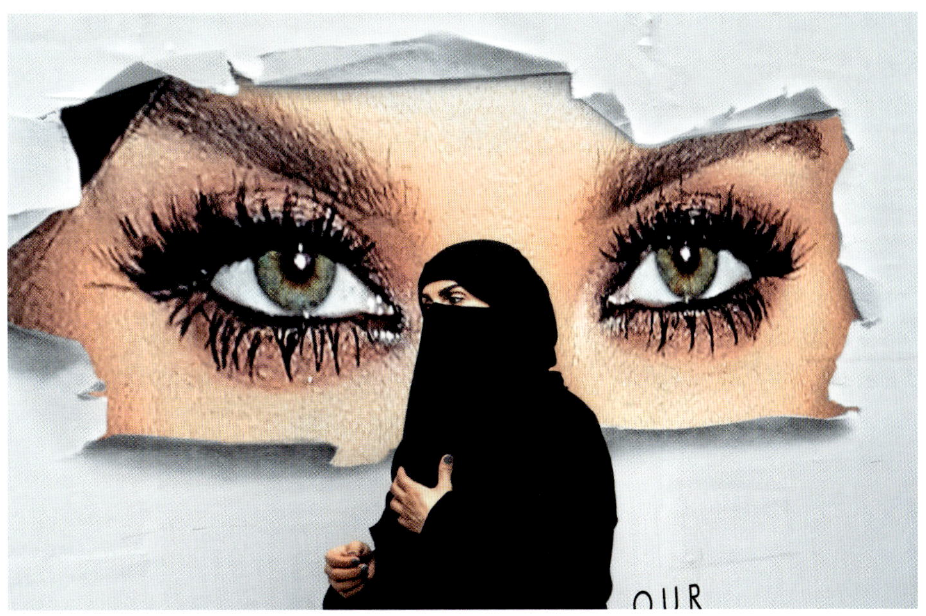

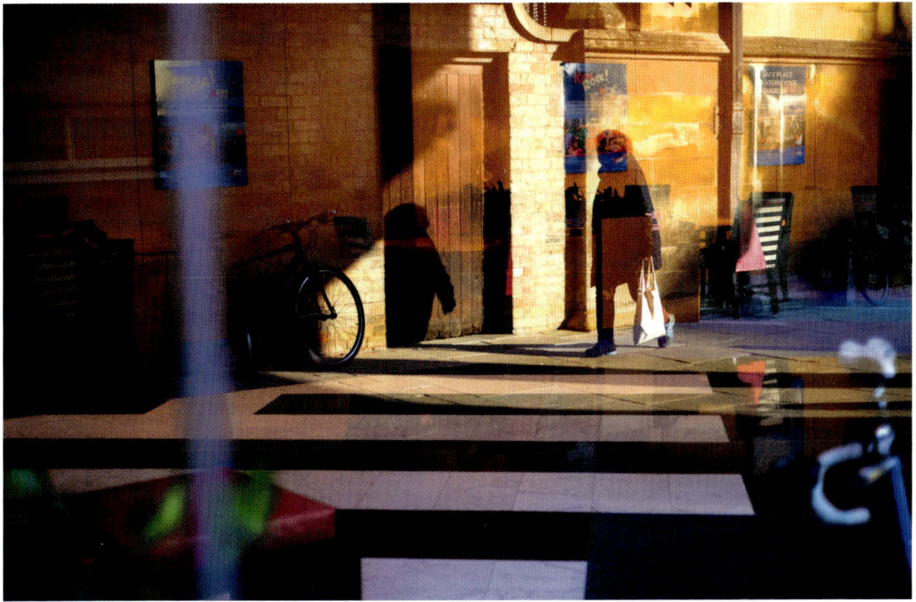

Find an advert or stretch of street that speaks to you and play with scenarios in your head.
ABOVE London, 2017
BELOW Cambridge, 2018

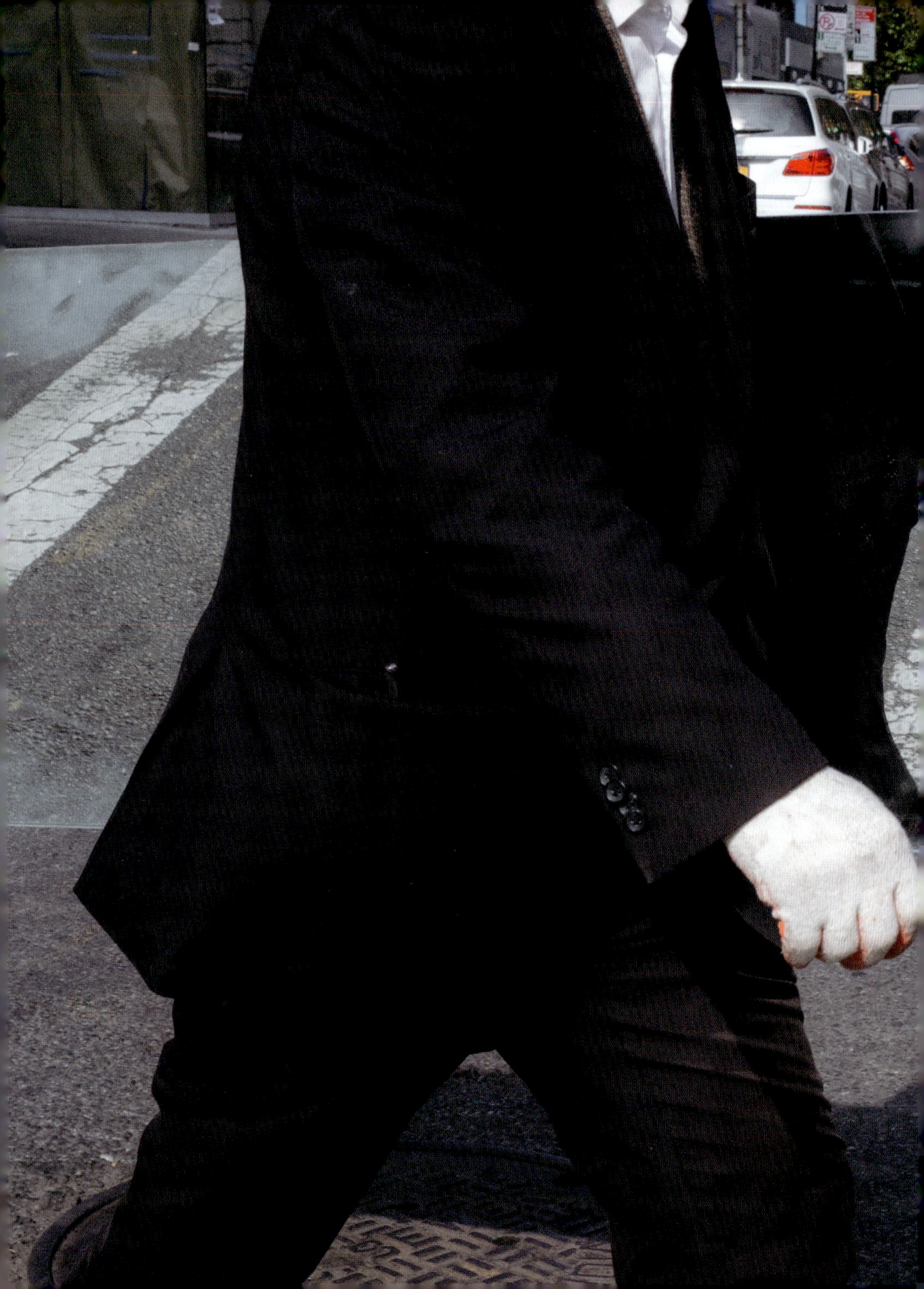

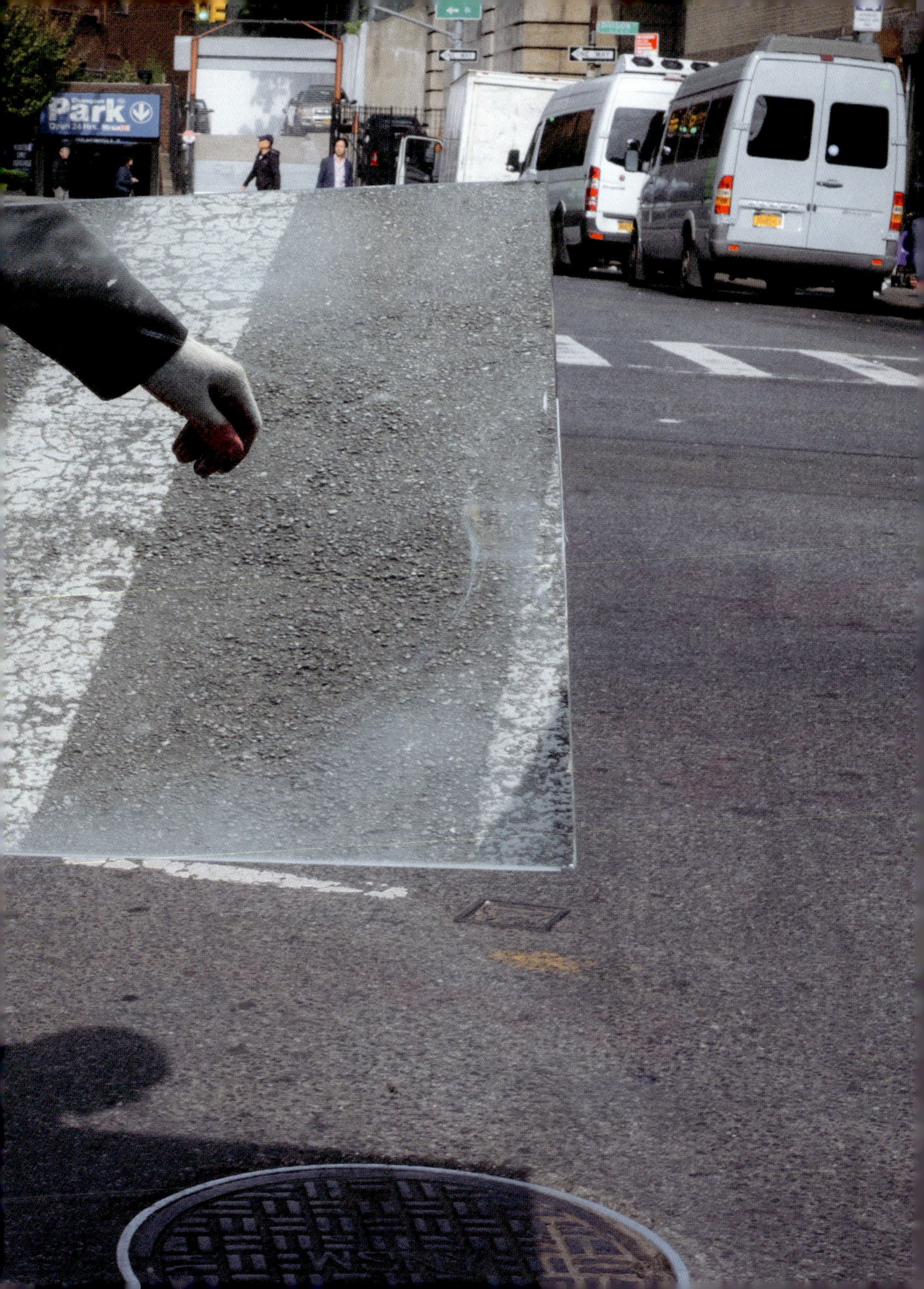
Park
24 Hrs
DIVISION
ONE WAY

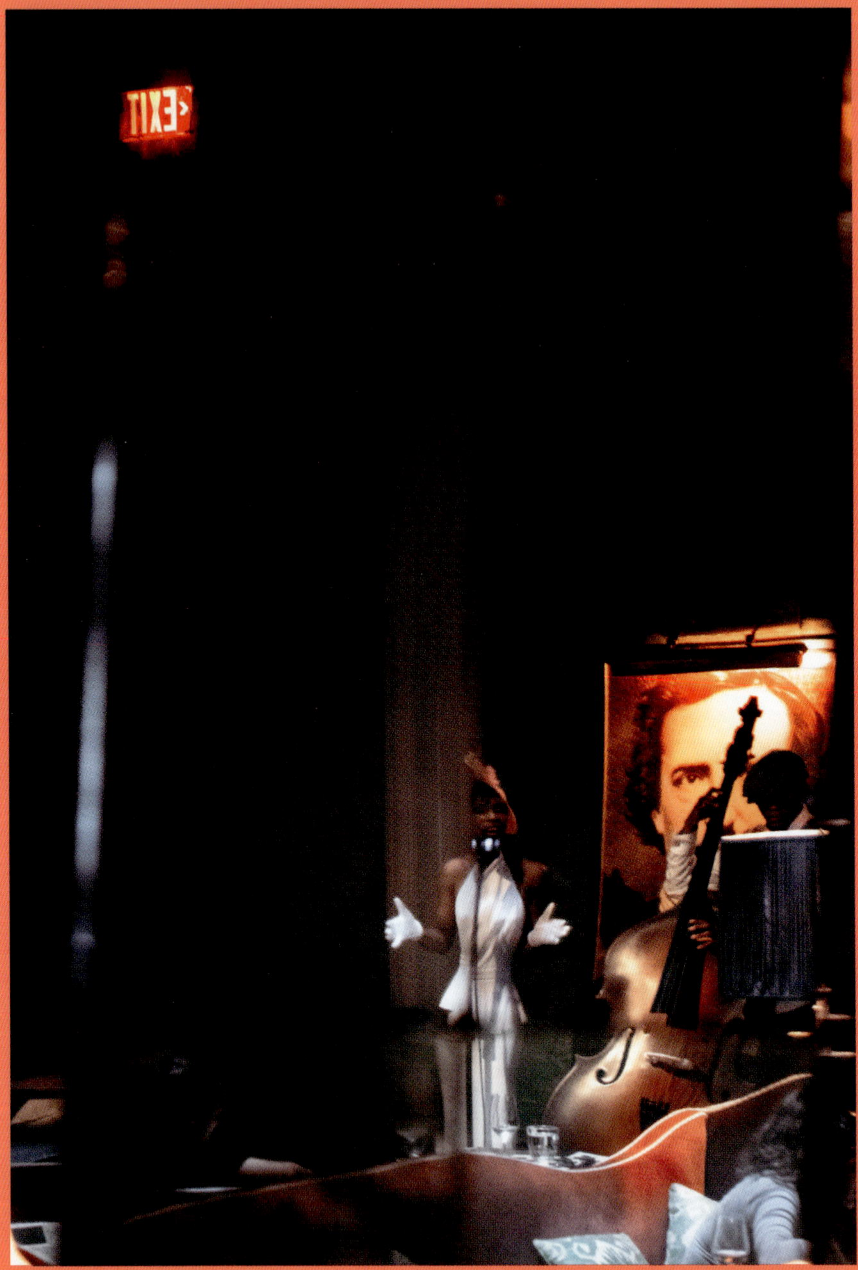

Are there visual cues that could place this image in a particular time period – or not?
New York, 2019

9

See in retrospect

Give your work staying power by featuring indicators of the present that may soon be past

Sometimes I think the smartphone is the curse of the contemporary street photographer because I like my images to have a kind of timeless quality. This is why I love umbrellas, and I'm not the only one. Many street photographers love shooting in the rain, because people put their phones away. They have their hands full, they're doing things, moving at a quicker pace, there's activity...

Don't get me wrong, a photograph in which a smartphone makes an appearance can still be a good picture. There's no reason to ignore them completely – after all, they are a feature of life today. You might be working in low light and take a nice shot where the phone screen is lighting up someone's face. That's something that just wouldn't have happened before the 2000s. But someone standing on the street, just looking at their phone, isn't interesting. There needs to be more... It could be that they're looking at something interesting and it's reflected in their glasses. There's a big university

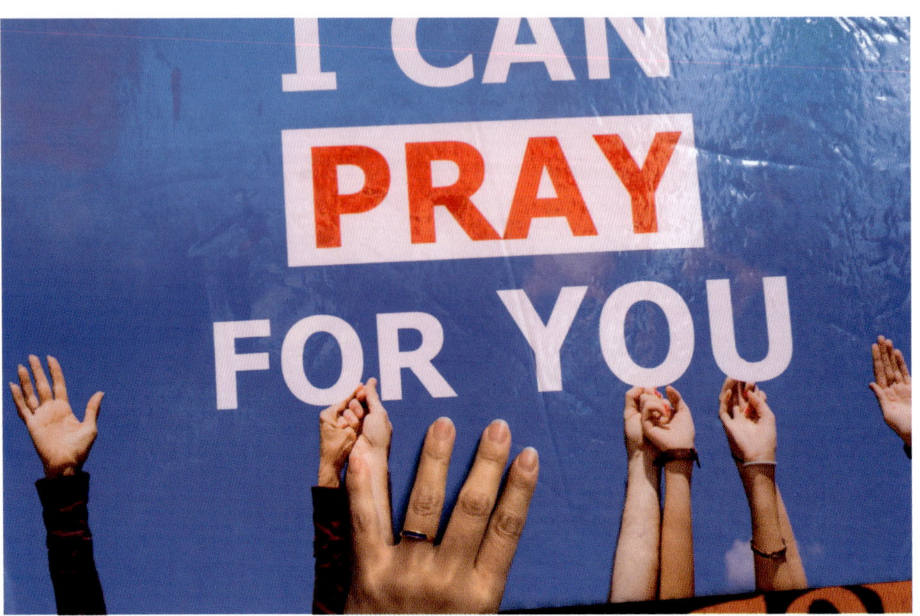

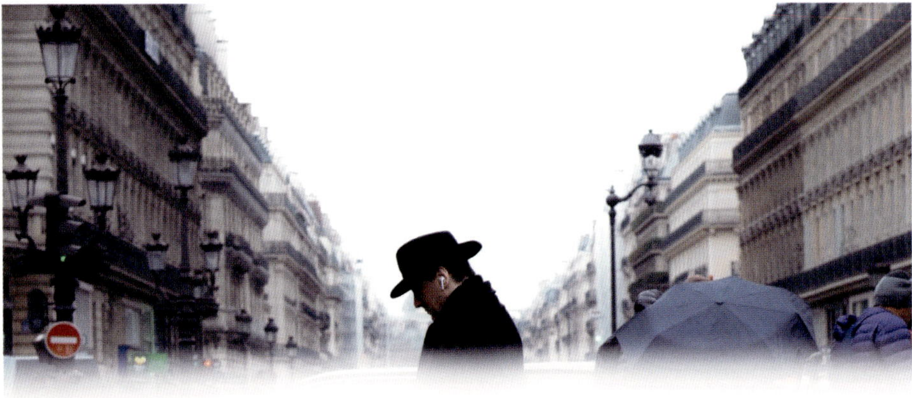

These shots have a historical relevance that comes from looking at them as if from the future.
ABOVE New York, 2018
BELOW Paris, 2018

campus near me and a few times passing by, I've spotted five, six, seven people all in a line, all with exactly the same body language – head tilted down, neck bent over, on their phones – although I'm yet to get a shot of it.

That's interesting because it shows a pattern of behaviour that is characteristic of our time. Try to look at the scenes in front of you through an imaginary future viewfinder. Ask yourself, what someone 10 or 50 years from now would notice if they were looking at this shot. To go back to smartphones, a single shot of a person with their phone is nothing! There are countless similar shots from the 1990s to the present day. It's only interesting if the person themself is interesting. Are they wearing something typical of that time? Are they carrying an oversized boombox? Technology and fashion, along with street signage, are guaranteed to look retro quickly. Although this isn't at the forefront of my work, it's something I consciously look out for, especially if I can use it in subtle ways, like in my 2018 shot of a man in a dark trilby hat marching through Paris, surrounded by 19th-century architecture, and with first-generation Apple AirPods just visible in his ears.

In a way, I'm thinking about the long-term significance of an image. It might be looked back on and seen as valuable even if it's something that I don't care about now. Maybe when I'm gone, it's the kind of image that might make it into a book one day because it shows such a stark contrast to the way things have turned out. I've got a whole bunch of shots from Times Square, of people holding up placards with religious slogans on them. There is one where someone is holding a placard saying 'Jesus can help' in front of an advert featuring a guy asking for help to fund a new kidney. In another one, a woman is holding a sign with lots of raised arms on it. Her fingers are the same size as one of these little arms. At the time, I just thought it looked funny. But who knows what'll happen in the future? The political climate might change and then it will have a different meaning. In the UK, the government is in the process of restricting protest in public spaces – perhaps there will come a time when we never see that again.

It's the same as people smoking on a plane. Once commonplace, this seems really weird now. You need to develop

'Try to look at the scenes in front of you through an imaginary future viewfinder.'

a sense of what might evolve. Cities are always shape-shifting.
That's what makes them such a magnet for photographers. There's
a photograph of the flagship HMV store in London's Oxford Street
that street photographer Stephen Leslie took in 2018. It shows a man
standing outside the grand store in the snow, wearing a bowler hat
and a dapper coat. Above him, is the classic HMV sign. Leslie took
another shot of the store, using exactly the same frame, in 2022.
With HMV now long gone, the shop is now a lowly sweet shop and all
that's left of the former grandeur is a flash of colour from the old sign.

If you went to the West End of London and took a lazy shot
of someone just standing there, in five years' time it would look
different. But there'll be plenty of shots like that. To ensure your
images stand the test of time, try to propose something interesting,
something that nobody else will have seen or done. Make them
work harder.

'Ask yourself, what someone 10 or 50 years from now would notice if they were looking at this shot.'

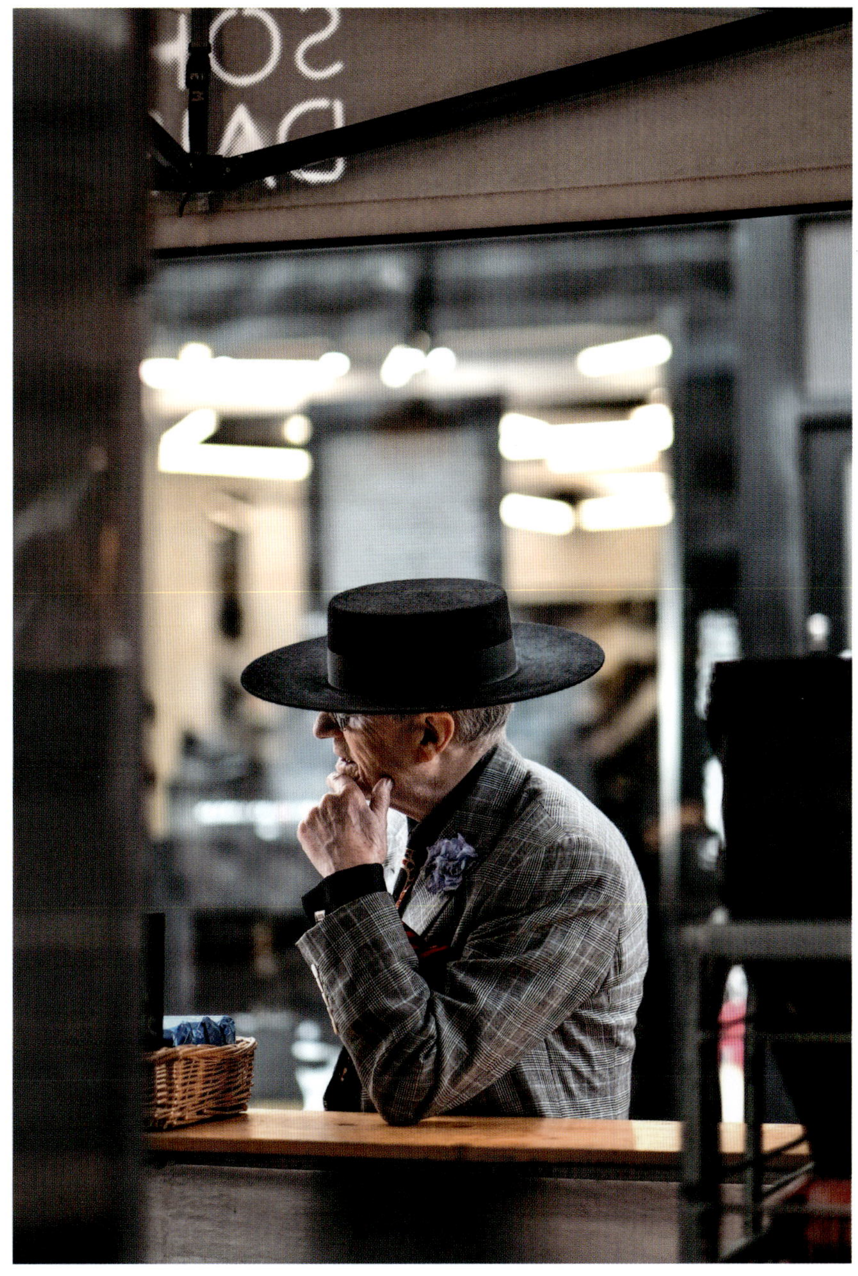

Don't take your city for granted. In a flash, it will change and so will its characters.
London, 2017

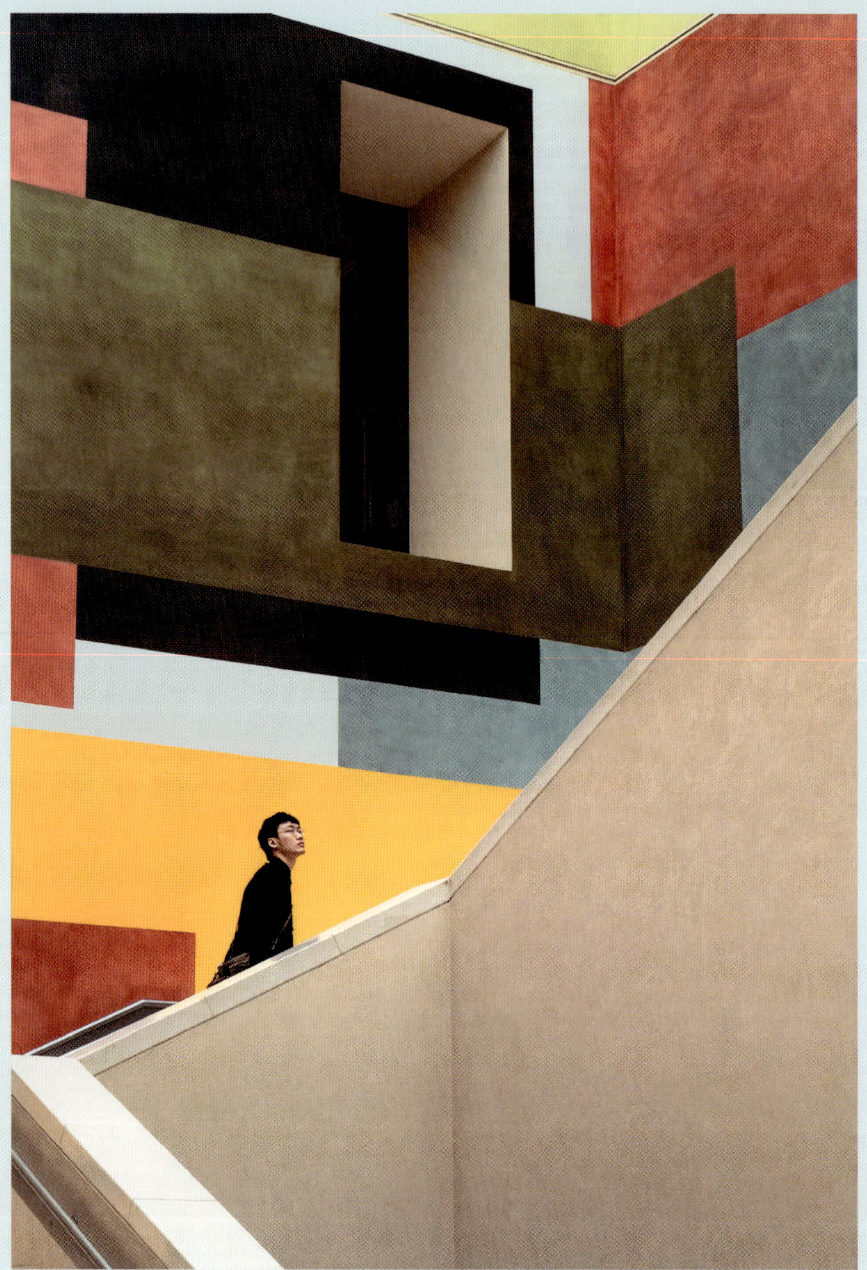

Composing an image is about arranging elements to inform viewers where their eyes should go.
London, 2017

10

Own your shot

Decide what your image is focused on and use your composition to take the viewer there

Just because you're a candid photographer, that doesn't mean you're passively observing the world around you. The four edges of your frame – where you situate them in relation to what you are looking at, how you line up what's inside them – represent your creative choices. More than anything else, composition is what makes or breaks a photograph. An interesting event poorly composed is nothing. It's wasted. A mundane moment could become extraordinary in the hands of a photographer with a trained eye. So, get to grips with the basics of composition and use these tools to send your viewer on a visual journey.

A quick Google search throws up pages of articles telling you the 'rules of composition'. There are hundreds of them. The principle behind them all is that, instead of simply framing up a subject dead centre (although this sometimes works – all rules are there to be broken), you give careful thought to directing someone's

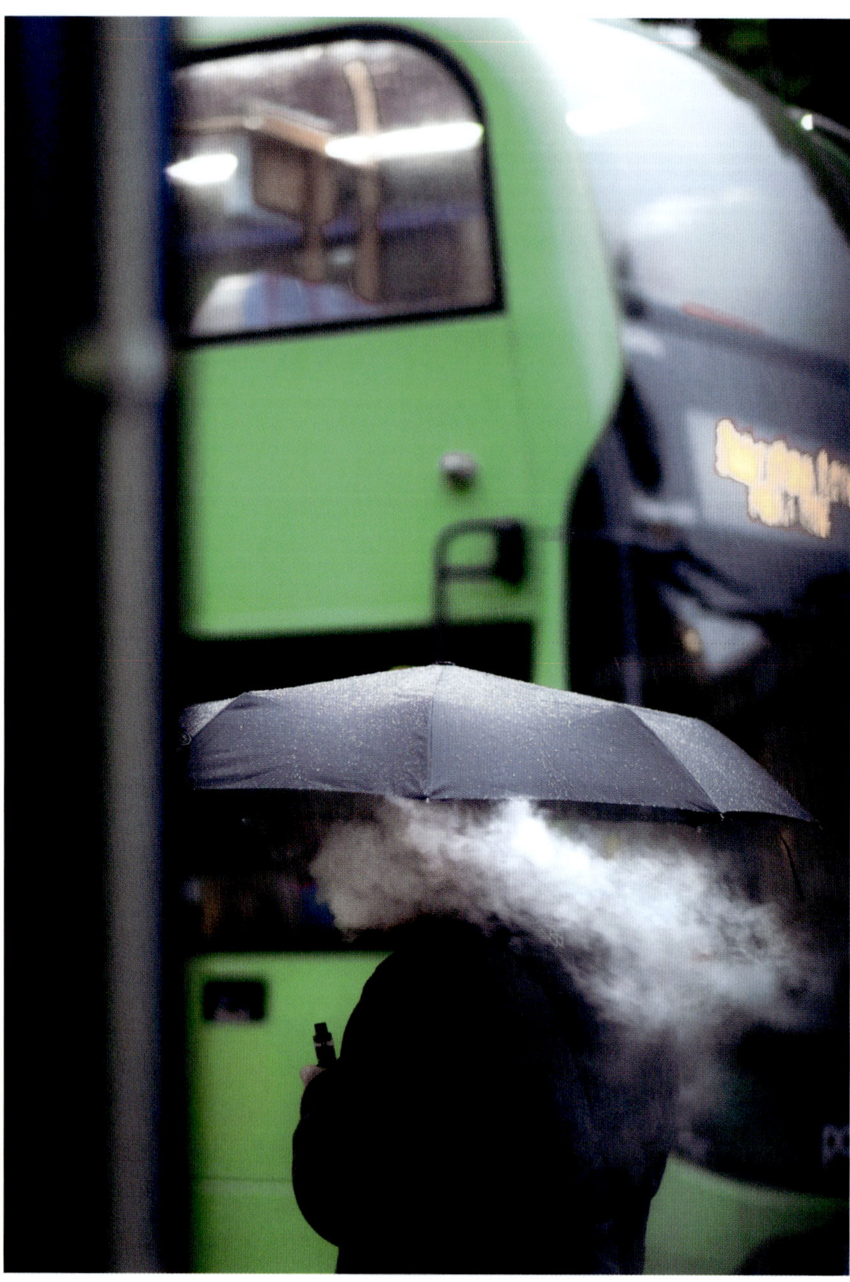

Use buildings, figures or vehicles – like this bus – to break up the frame into segments.
Cambridge, 2018

eye around a frame so that they see what you consider to be the most important element. Good composition is also about giving a picture a feeling of balance, so it just intuitively looks right. My shots don't tend to 'tell a story', but I do like to create intrigue and this is how I do that. 'Leading lines', for example, is about using the lines in a scene to point the viewer's gaze to the main subject – they may be architectural or created by the movement of people's bodies or the shape of the landscape.

'More than anything else, composition is what makes or breaks a photograph.'

Start off by setting yourself a challenge each day to make an image using a particular rule. In time, you'll find there are rules that naturally chime with you and you'll use them without a second thought. Or maybe you'll look back through your archive and notice that you always use the 'rule of thirds' or the 'rule of odds' unconsciously. I have a shot, for instance, that shows the edge of an old, red Routemaster London bus that fills most of the frame. I could have achieved a cleaner composition, but I deliberately included this edge because it leads you down the image towards where the subject is, a man, almost silhouetted in the frame of the bus window. There's another leading line that takes you across the image the other way. Sometimes a little bit of imperfection is great if it does what you need.

Pretty consistently, I make a similar type of composition, where there's maybe a quarter or a third of the frame blocked out by something on the near side. It's almost always because there's just an ugly element in the frame that I don't like, or I'm at a junction and deliberately blocking out the street to my right by hiding around the corner. I'm always looking to simplify scenes to create minimalist, unusual images where colour, light and shapes dominate. People often make a composition too obvious by focusing on the – usually human – subject. Say you're walking down the street following a great subject that isn't going to disappear suddenly. The street's maybe 100m (300ft) long, so you have plenty of time to make all the necessary decisions and compose your shot. If you don't want the street to feature in the image, you don't have to include it. It's that simple. It's your choice what you do and don't include.

Don't feel limited by what you find in front of you. There are so many elements around a street. You can use anything to obscure distractions – hoarding, lampposts, even other people. Working in the same small place day in, day out, you can block out identifiable elements to create different images. Longer lenses are ideal for that. The longer the lens you use, the more you can focus on little details, and the more this brings out in your foreground. I don't see a long lens necessarily as a way of getting closer, I see it as a creative tool. It means I can include multiple layers between me and the thing I want to photograph. I am always trying to get the best version of the image, doing as much editing of the content as possible in-camera.

A picture I took of some kids sitting on a swing installation at London's Tate Modern is a good illustration of how I compose. There are four different lines from a pole, a railing, the swing's structure and the building. Together they produce a box around the children, which leads in a spiral towards them in the centre. The viewer is being completely drawn around the frame. This demonstrates how I use 'leading lines' as well as sub-framing, which I'll discuss in more detail later (see Chapter 12). In this situation, I found the frame first. Apart from that spot, the scene was messy, so I composed the shot before anyone ever sat down. The installation was in the middle of Tate Modern and people had been shooting there loads while it was up. But no one had got anything really good. I knew my shot represented the cleanest version of the entire area, so I just framed up and waited until the picture came.

Understanding the rules is a great place to start. After a while, you'll be taking pictures and everything will feel right, and the reason it feels right is because you're following some kind of rule. It doesn't matter how you get there when you're starting out – you can just shoot interesting moments and then crop in post. This way, you can move the image around to make it fit the rule and help you better understand it for the next time you're out shooting. Either option is going to work. At the beginning, you don't want to think about everything at once. You'll probably be figuring out exposure

'A mundane moment could become extraordinary in the hands of a photographer with a trained eye.'

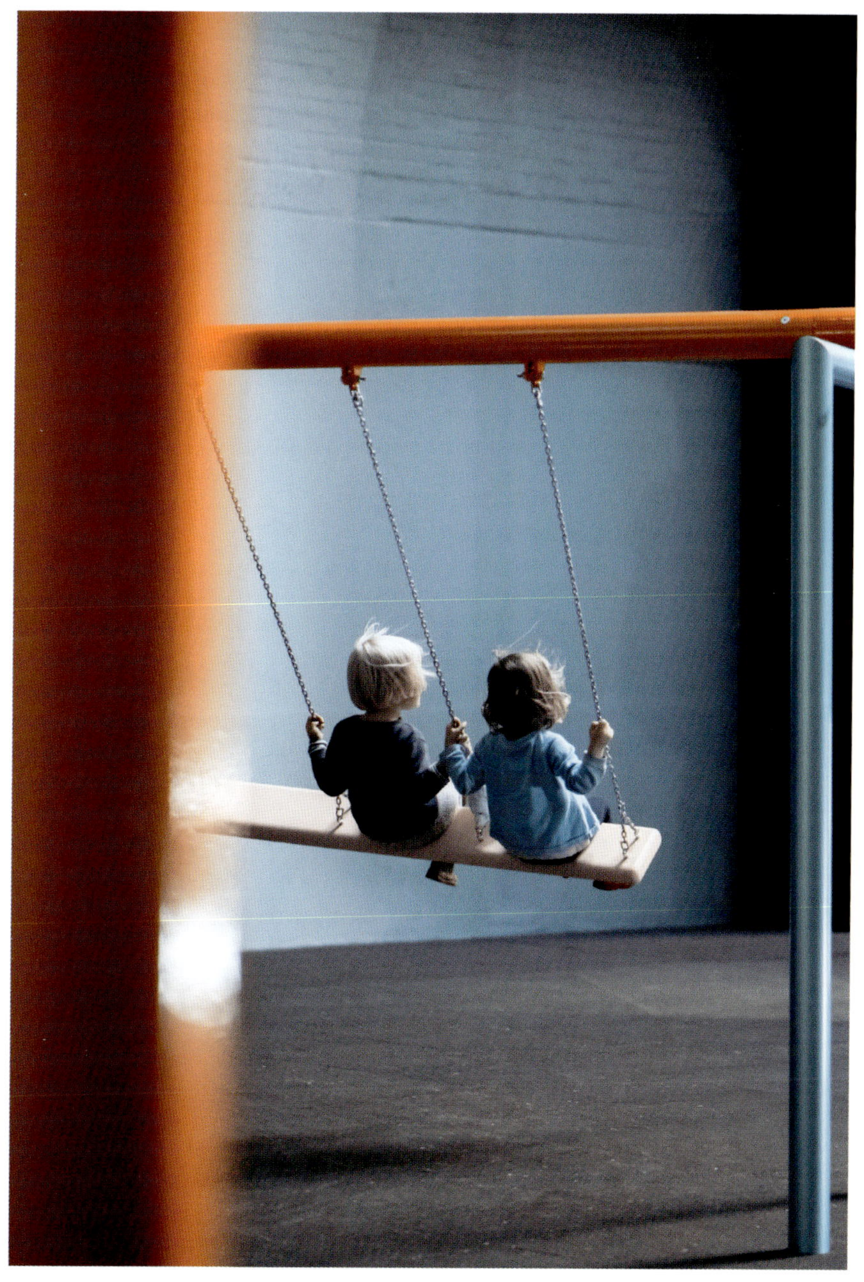

By selectively isolating the swing within my frame, I produced a more interesting image.
London, 2017

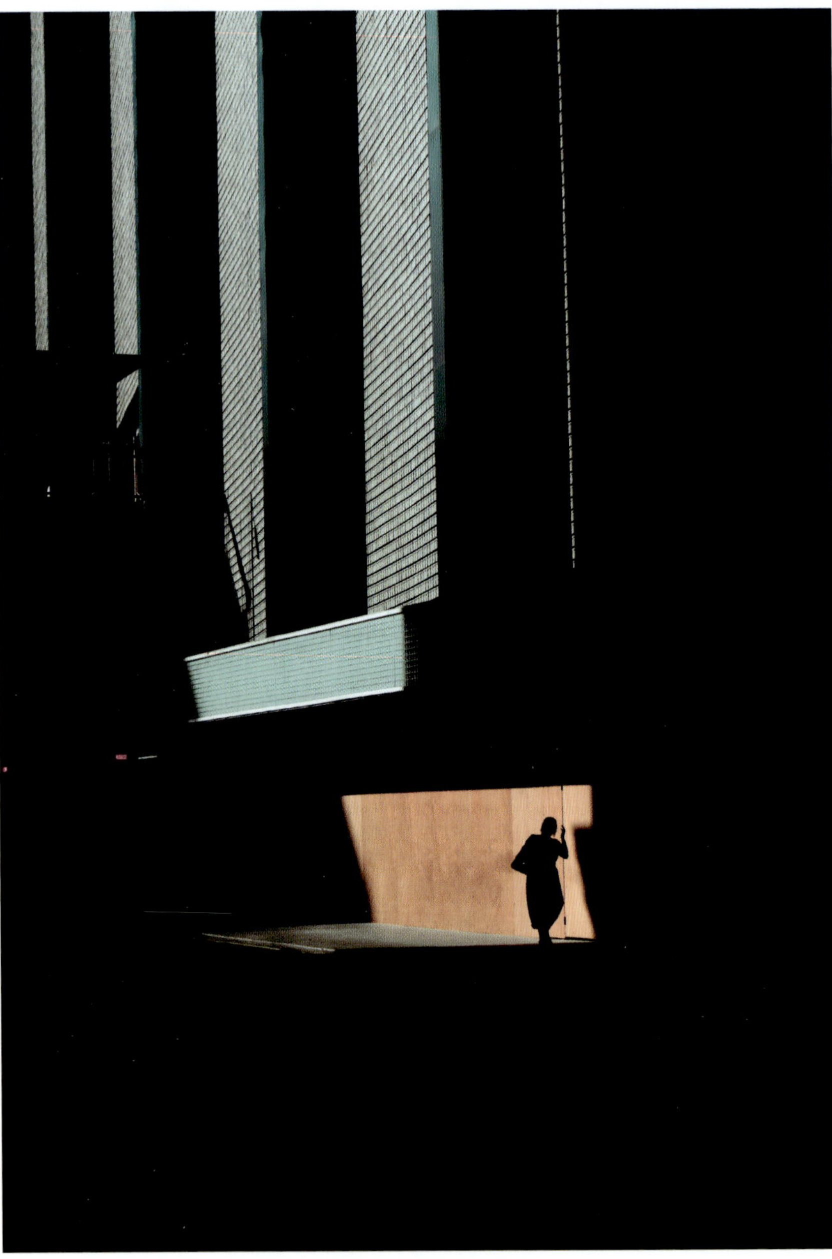

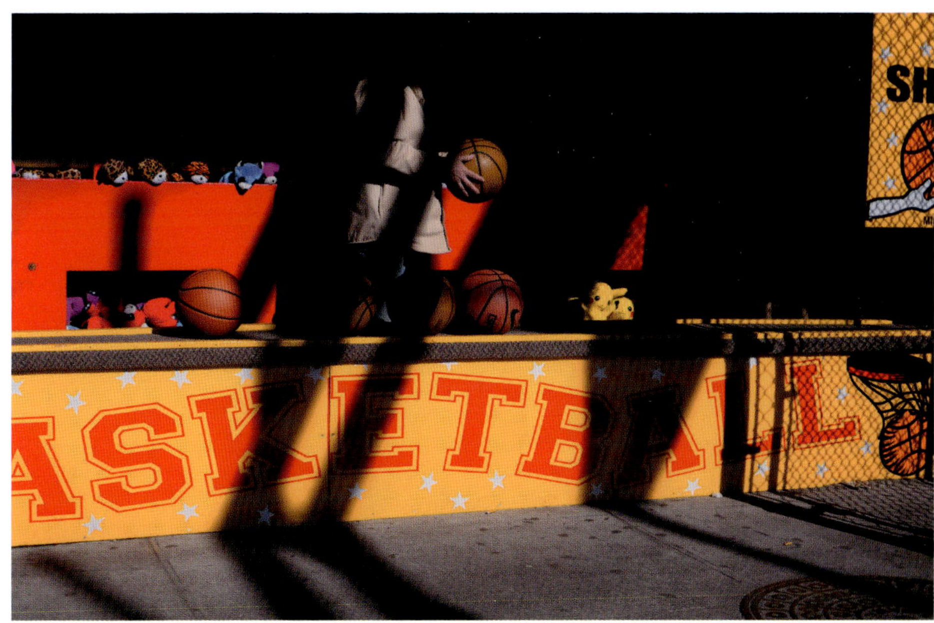

and how your camera works. You'll be looking for moments, you'll be looking for colour – there'll be so much going on, that some of the decisions fall by the wayside.

Eventually, however, you will find yourself gravitating towards certain rules. For me it's the rule of thirds. I didn't set out to use it but, over time, I've come to realise that it's in many of my images. You'll do the same. You'll be thinking about a few of the rules and trying to compose like that. And then one day, you'll take an image you really love. Then you'll dissect it to find out why it works so well. Maybe it's because there are five subjects in the frame and it fits the 'rule of odds'. Maybe there's a bright red element off-centre and it's that colour that attracts you. People don't often take the time to sit back and take their images apart like that. But if you do, you'll make the connection. You'll discover what it is that makes your work distinctive. And then you'll see images you like wherever you go.

Photography is about dark, as well as light. In these compositions, shadow guides the eye.

LEFT
London, 2021

ABOVE
New York, 2018

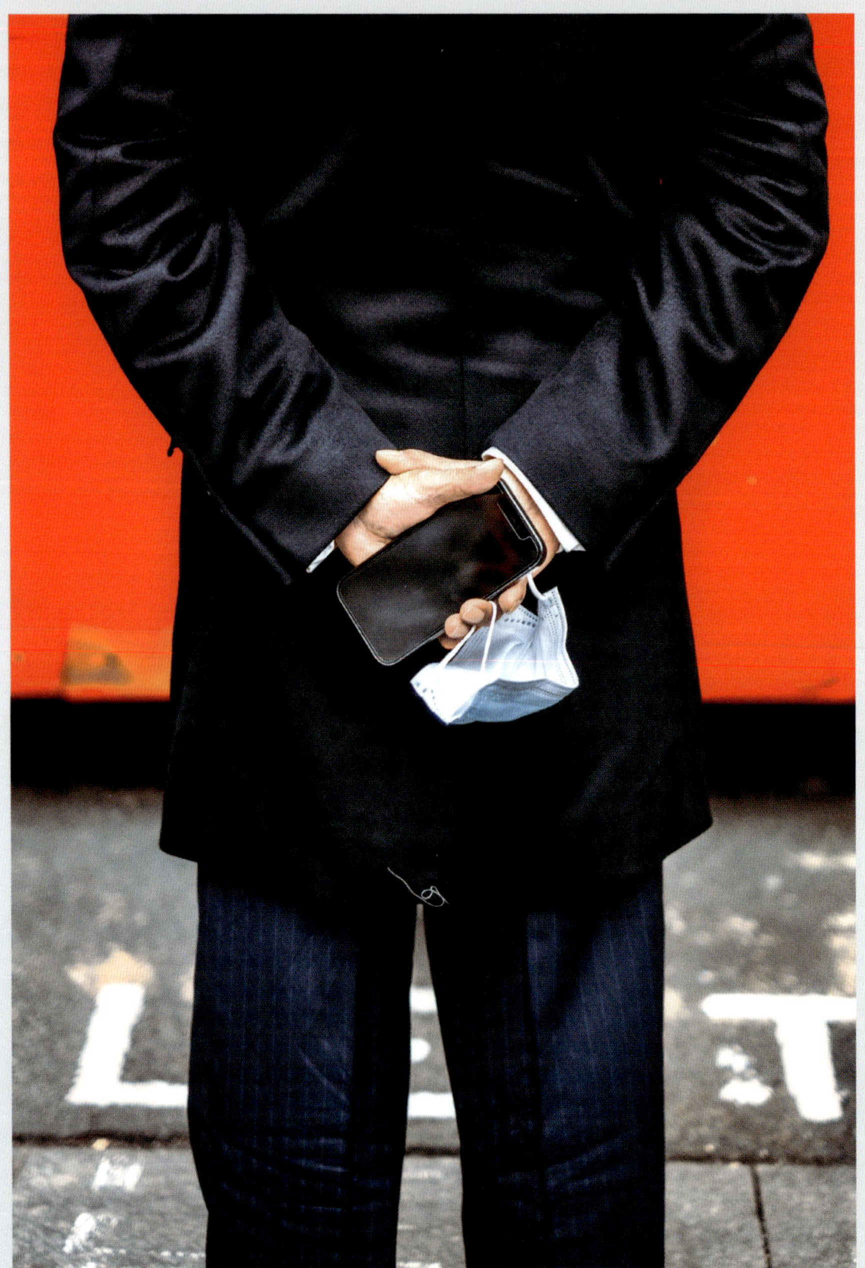

Suit, smartphone – and medical facemask. Contradictions can make an image stand out.
London, 2021

11

Contrast to intrigue

Engage the viewer with striking juxtapositions

There's a shot I took in London of a guy dressed up and looking really dapper. The top half of the frame is entirely red because a bus is passing in front of him. He's got his hands behind his back and looks exactly like a character you might see in an old Vivian Maier shot from the middle of the last century. Except that he's got a smartphone clasped in his hand and a medical facemask hanging off his fingers. These little anchors root the image in the present. But it's the contrast between them and his timeless attire that gives it the edge. Cambridge, the city where I live and shoot most of the time, is steeped in tradition – historic college buildings from as far back as the 1200s, academics or students donning gowns and mortarboards for graduation ceremonies. That's not my focus. But if I see someone dressed in an old-fashioned three-piece suit with headphones hanging out of their fancy waistcoat, I'm interested.

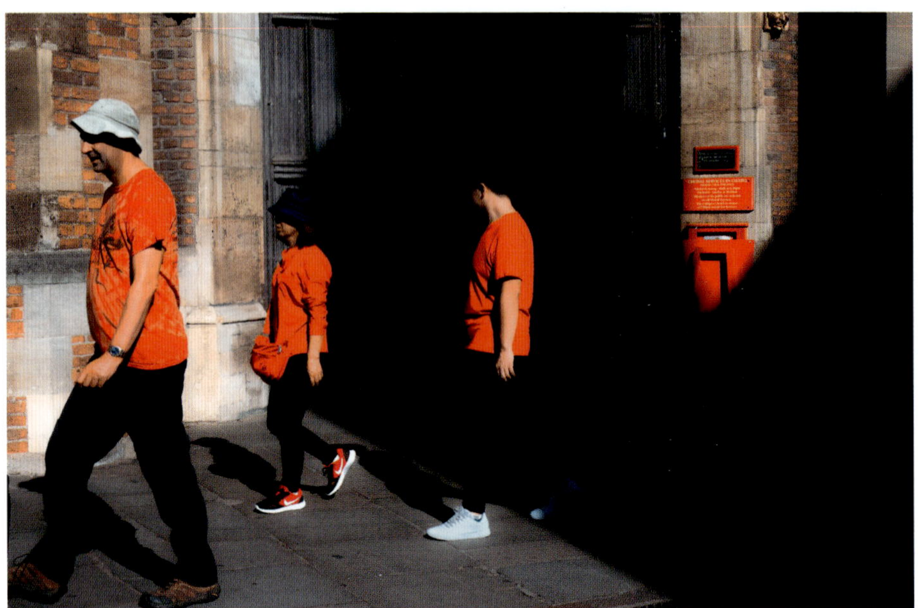

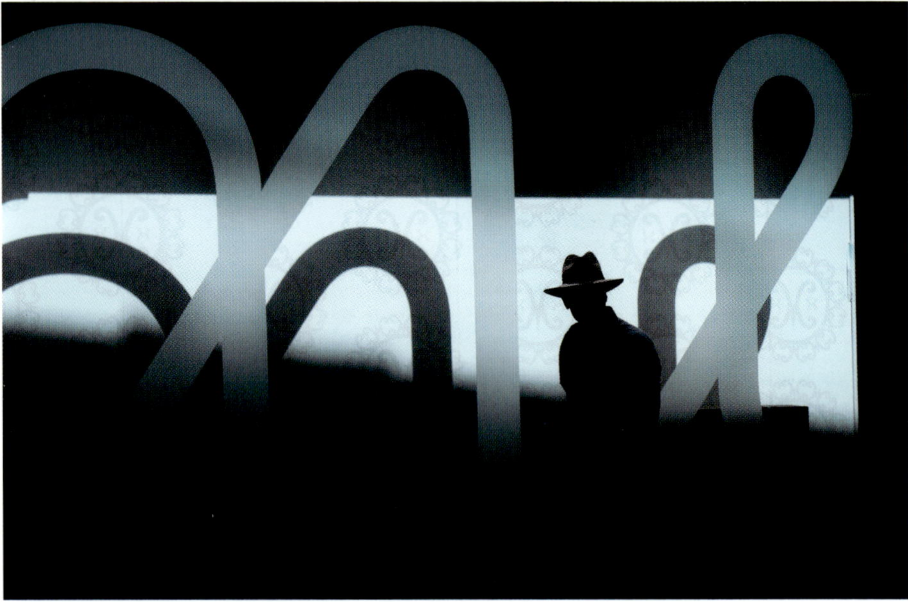

We look because we are curious. Images like these pose more questions than they answer.
ABOVE Cambridge, 2018
BELOW Cambridge, 2021

     Find Your Frame

Juxtaposition creates intrigue. My images don't work by spelling out a whole narrative – what they do instead is to alert the viewer's curiosity and make them ask questions. You don't only have to look at people, their clothes or their behaviour, to find this. The most basic form of contrast at your disposal is light and shadow. I'm always looking at that first and foremost and you'll notice that I use silhouettes regularly in my pictures for this reason. One example is an image from July 2021. I shot it in Cambridge, but it could be anywhere, because the content of the image is so stripped back. It shows a man in a hat against a band of light in the middle of the frame, with looping patterns from the window of Virgin Bank, which was in the process of undergoing a refit, also shooting out shadows around him. It's a very minimalist, graphic picture, but if you're dealing with something busier, try switching your camera settings to monochrome. That way you'll be able to see more clearly whether a particular composition offers interesting intersections between bright and dark areas.

'Speculate about the best scenario for making a shot and play it out in your head.'

The advantage of working with colour is that it offers you a wider range of elements to play with when you're creating juxtaposition. There are times when including or excluding the tiniest snatch of colour can make or break an image. You can direct someone's eye around a frame by contrasting one colour with another. Other times, the juxtaposition is actually a repetition – the striped jumper a woman is wearing that echoes the stripes of some shutters she is strolling past, say, or someone's scarlet nail polish that picks up the bright red of the rail an anonymous Tube passenger is leaning against. A hypothetical composition I had teed up for a while came to fruition in a 2018 shot that shows a set of people all in red walking past a red postbox in Cambridge. I had earmarked the post box, as I love the colour red and knew that it would make a great shot if I could bring other red elements into the frame. It was a real touch to capture these passers-by as a group because they weren't actually together. The man was on his own, walking much faster than the other two people. It was fortuitous for me that the timing worked out to position them that way.

Many street photographers like a witty juxtaposition, usually involving humans. The best-known example of this type of shot is dubbed 'balloon head' – someone, most likely a child, is holding a balloon which somehow ends up completely obscuring their face and it looks as if the balloon is their head. No doubt that's an image you've come across a few times. To make your images stand out, you need to push that concept further, do something original. There is an image of mine showing some kids on the top deck of a bus. The windows are steamed up and the kids are amusing themselves by drawing pictures in the condensation. By coincidence, just underneath them there's an advertisement for the 2017 Matt Damon movie *Downsizing*, which features the words 'miniature masterpiece'. Now, that's the definition of a one-off moment but it's also something that you could predict might happen once you'd seen the advert and the steamed windows. Without those words, the image would have fallen flat.

When you're walking your usual routes around the city, keep your eyes peeled for things that you could use to create interesting juxtapositions. Maybe there's a billboard or some digital screens featuring some text or an image – the words 'look up', for example, or a set of eyes or some lips. With text, you can almost edit on the spot by framing up, so that you cut out certain words and focus on those that are relevant. Speculate about the best scenario for making a shot using this and play it out in your head. Maybe it's a particular kind of person, or a person moving their body in a certain way. If you have these in mind, you can hang around or return sometime later in the hope that you'll be ready when the right person turns up.

Contrast and the 'rule of thirds' often go together. Juxtaposed elements can occupy different portions of the frame – by mentally breaking it up into constituent parts, you can give it punch through placement. A good way to finesse your technique is to find something interesting that you know isn't going anywhere, frame up

'My images alert the viewer's curiosity and make them ask questions.'

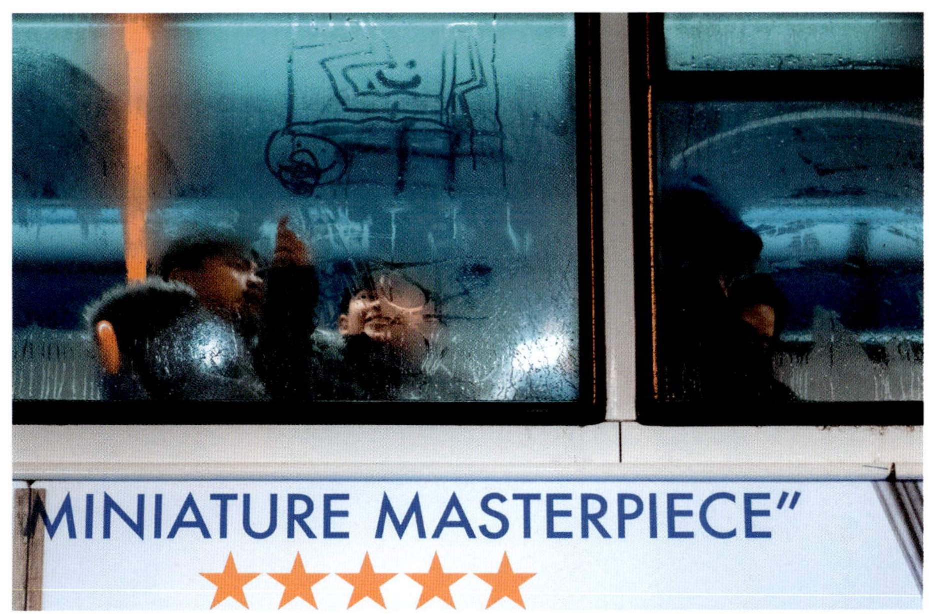

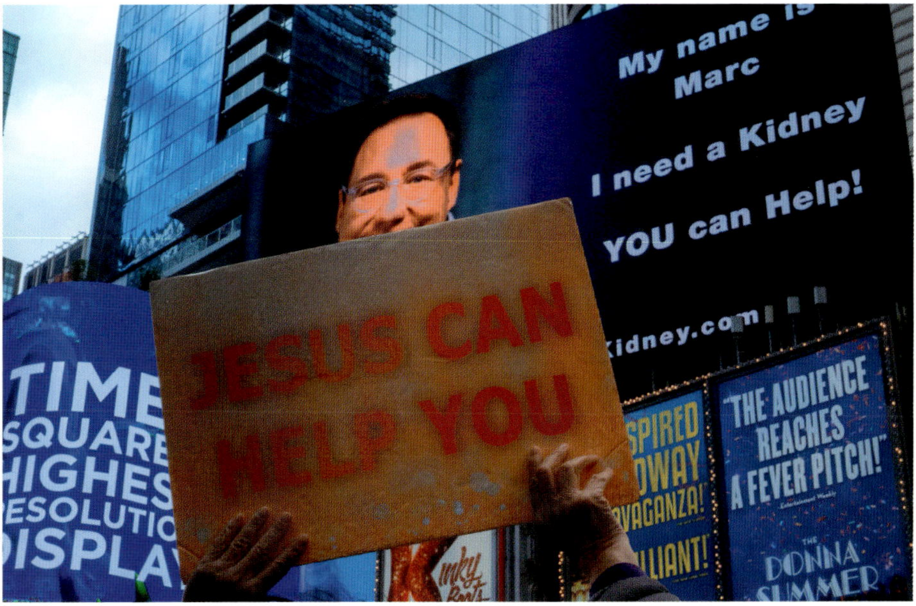

Cities are full of words. Experiment with adverts or placards to give your shots a witty edge.
ABOVE Cambridge, 2018
BELOW New York, 2018

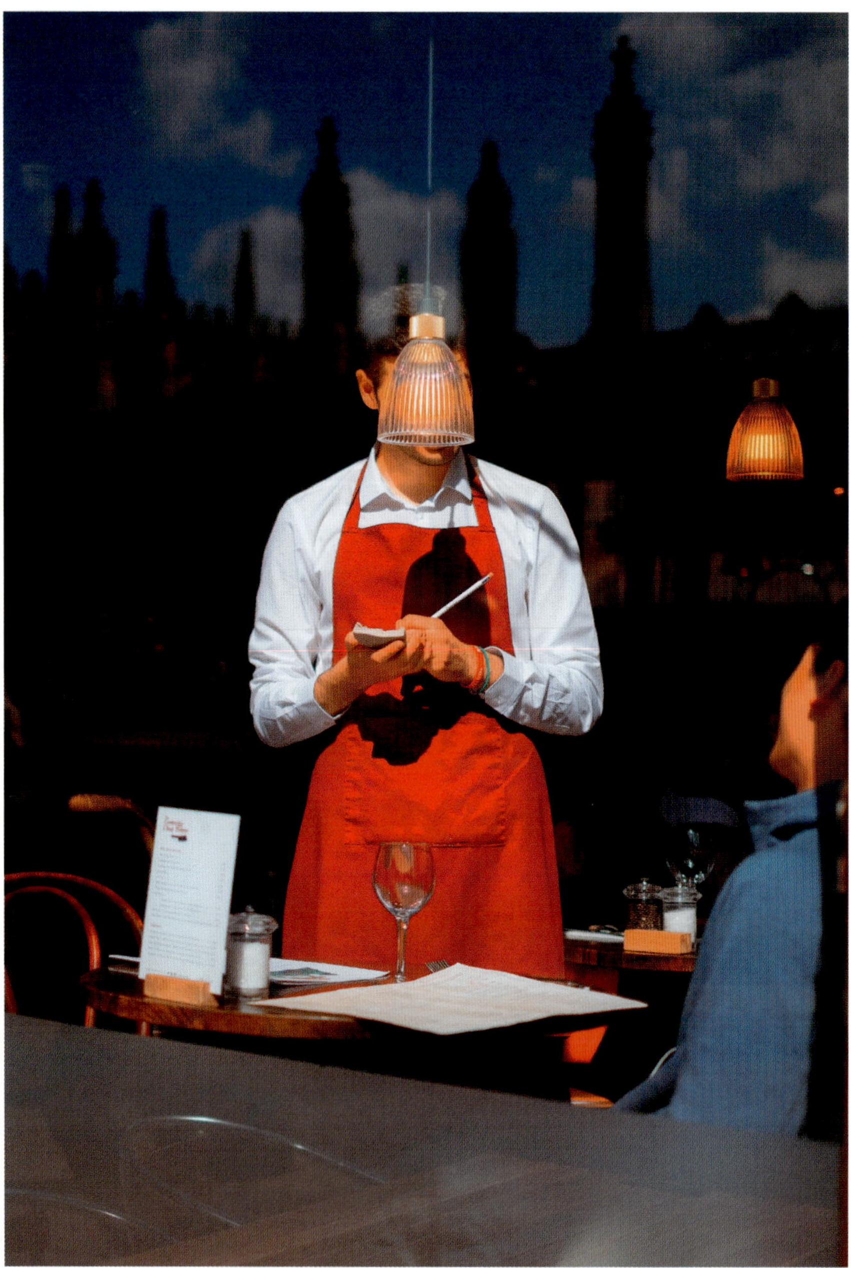

A playful variant of the classic 'balloon head', but here the balloon is a pendant lampshade.
Cambridge, 2019

and sit tight until your best-case scenario happens. I still do this myself. In Cambridge there's an advert for cosmetics where someone has stuck a white sticker over one eye. I keep returning to it, hoping someone with an eye patch will come past, but it hasn't happened yet. Another way to practise this is by looking back through shots you've already taken and think about what funny little elements would finish them off perfectly? Once you've got the hang of that, you can start to incorporate more unpredictable moving elements in your shots. Instead of having one person doing something surprising, you could get several, like in this shot of street food truck vendors giving directions to a customer – they all point in unison, neatly finished off with the word 'welcome'. Contrast conspires with every other component of a well-thought out composition to give your viewer a reason to look.

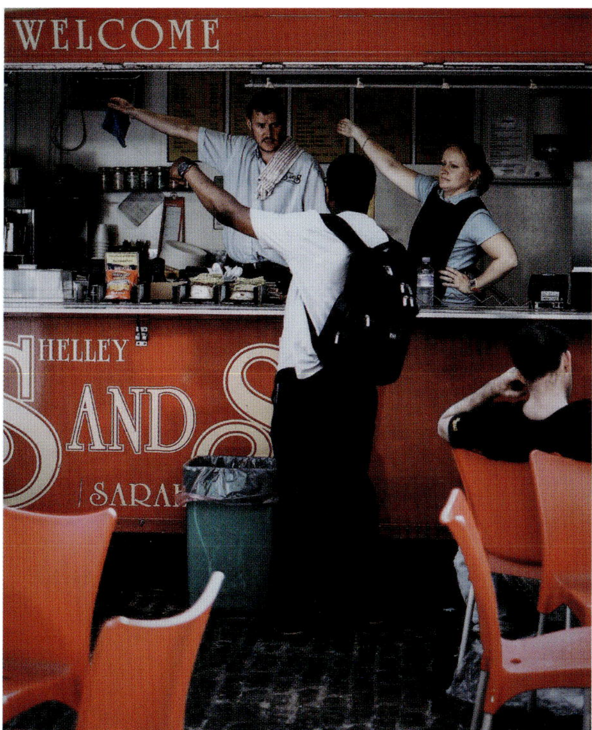

Asking for directions isn't itself unusual, but the sight of three people pointing is comic. Cambridge, 2006

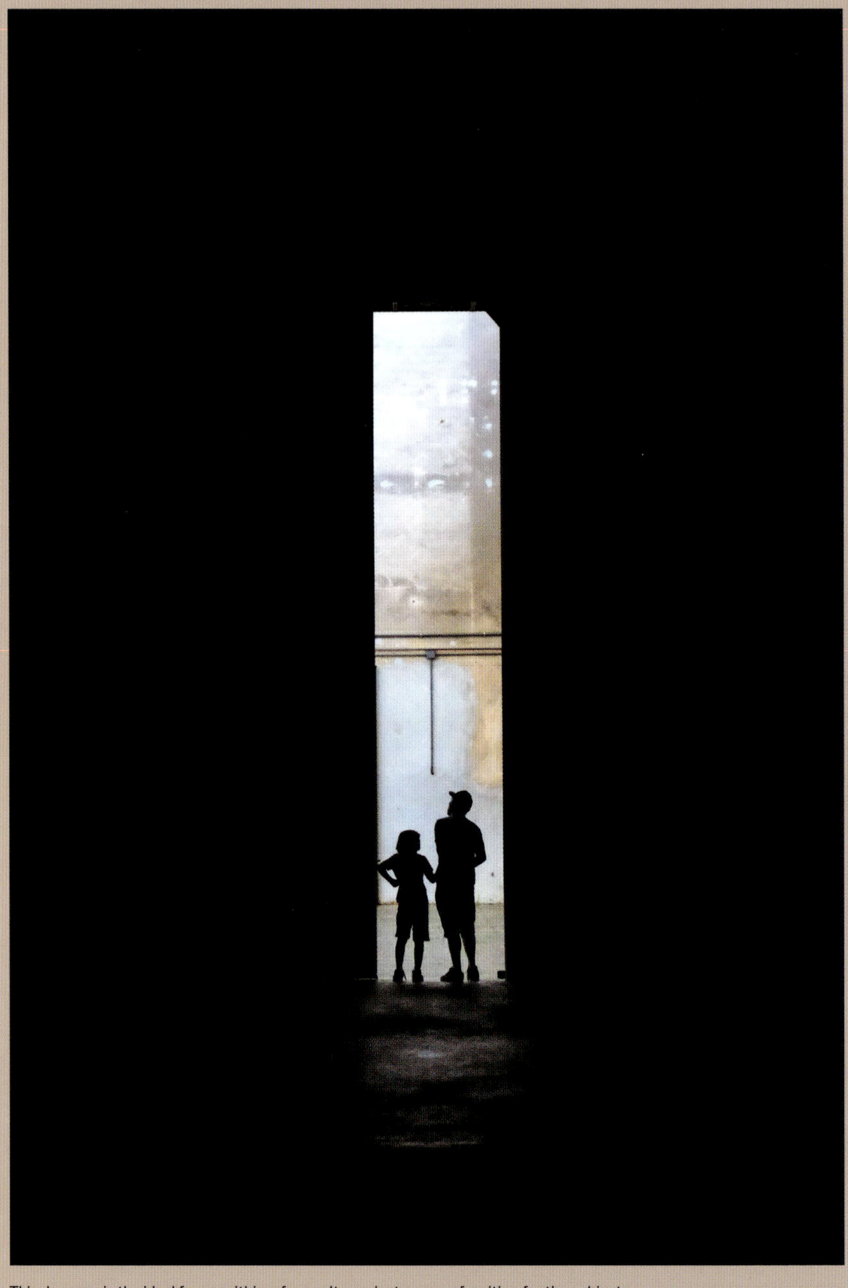

This doorway is the ideal frame within a frame. It was just a case of waiting for the subjects.
Milan, 2017

12

Frame within a frame

Make order out of chaos by boxing your subject in

Doors, windows, lampposts, shards of light – in a photograph, anything can become a sub-frame. I first came across this compositional technique looking at other people's work and it's one I use all the time. It's playful but also incredibly useful, offering a way to rid an image of unwanted visual clutter. For me, working in the same handful of streets most of the time, that's a necessity, a way to continue making images that look fresh, rather than showing the same scenes on repeat. At first, it became an obsession and now I do it without giving it a second thought. It's one of the reasons why I love rainy days. Umbrellas create nice shapes that move in and out of shot, giving you opportunities to create different sub-frames with them.

As with the 'balloon head' trope (see page 80), there is a basic version of sub-framing that involves photographing a person

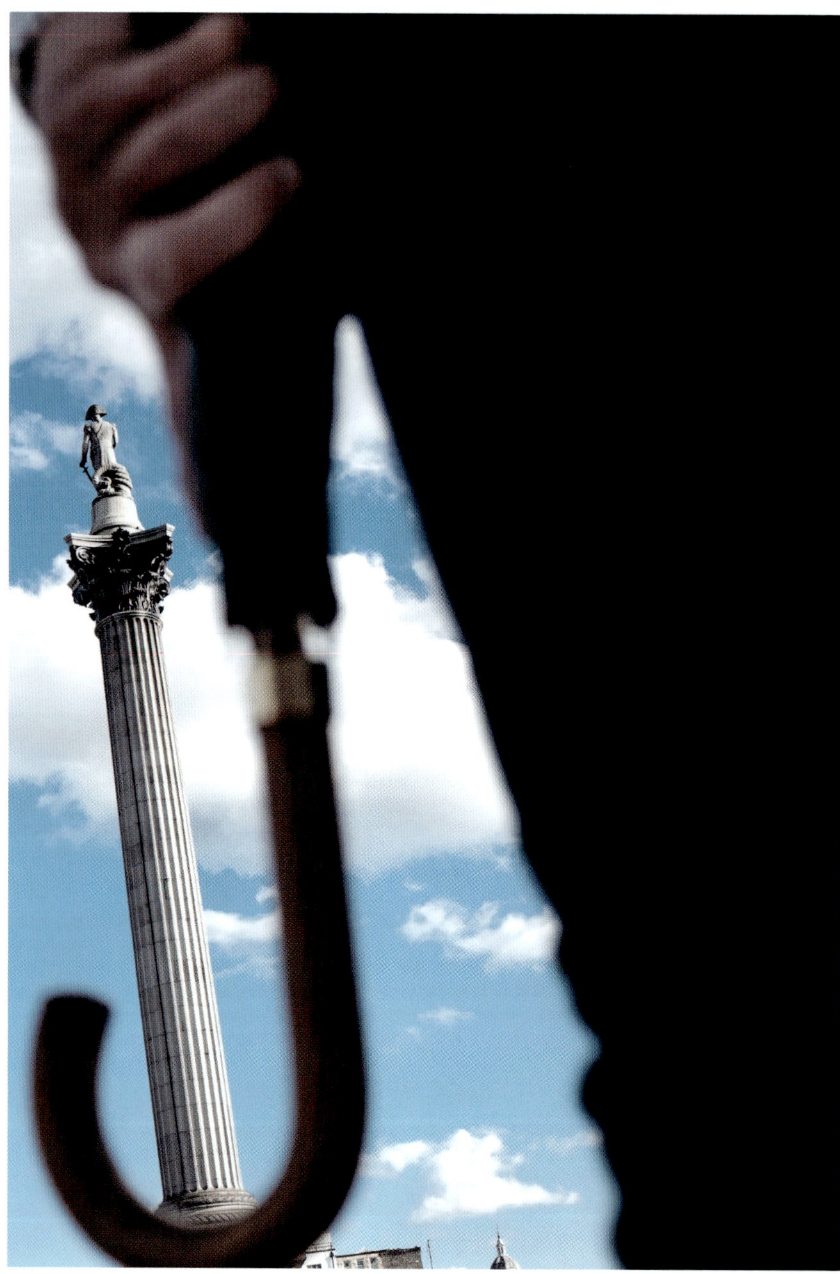

There's no limit to what you can use to sub-frame – this umbrella handle worked a treat.
London, 2017

through a window. It could be the open window of a café or a steamed-up car window. Doors have the same effect. Take an image I shot in 2017, in Pirelli HangarBicocca, an art gallery in Milan in a former industrial building. It shows two figures framed up in a tall doorway between two rooms within the gallery. That's an example of a sub-frame that's just given to you. If you had been in that spot and not taken the shot, I'm not sure what it is you'd have been looking at. I think it works so well because of the strong contrast. Everything is in darkness except for the doorway and there is something about the man and the child, the way they are standing, their gesture, that makes you curious. It may not be my most original shot, but it's certainly pleasing to look at.

Sometimes, as in that Milan shot, people are surrounded by the frame; other times, you can create the illusion of this by the way you position yourself when you take the picture. You can bring layers or other elements into the scene to block out certain portions of what you can see and give the appearance of a frame. There's a picture I took in Trafalgar Square, where you can see Nelson's Column against a blue sky broken up with fluffy clouds through the sub-frame of a man's umbrella handle. Nelson was my static element and I just waited until the man fortunately moved into the position where I could get the shot as I had imagined it. Another time, I was leading the participants of a workshop that I was running to another location when I chanced on this picture, where you can see a man's face perfectly framed in the mirror of his motorbike. Again, this was a case of thinking ahead and knowing that the only time someone's face is going to be positioned right in the mirror is if they're sitting on the bike. It's also a reminder never to put your camera away because you don't know what gems lie right around the corner.

I'll use anything to create a sub-frame. I've taken a picture of a market trader with his hands on his head, shooting through his arm to create a triangular frame. In another one, which took me several attempts, you can just see someone's face in a circular hole in a road sign. I spotted the sign in town, and knew that it wouldn't be of interest to anyone else. It was in a high traffic spot, so I knew someone would eventually stop where I needed them to be and

> ## 'Umbrellas create nice shapes that move in and out of shot, giving you opportunities to create different sub-frames with them.'

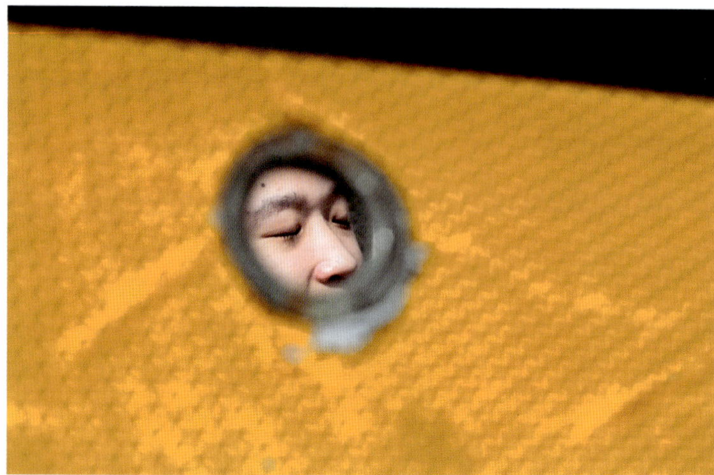

look round. I would have plenty of time to thread the needle.
After several 10-minute-long visits to the spot, someone did stop
and I had maybe 10 seconds to get the shot. This wouldn't work
with a wide-angle lens because it would bring in too much else.
That said, you can still sub-frame if you are working with a wide
angle; you just need to be bolder and bring in larger elements
to block out greater portions of the frame.

A good way to practise sub-framing is by framing a shot
as you would normally and then considering which elements you
could subtract to make it cleaner, the subject more contained.
Alternatively, go out and find 10 things in your city that would make
good sub-frames. Keep a note and take your chance when you see
a good subject heading for one of those frames. You can shoot
through corners of buildings, the space between a sign and a wall,
a bike stand. Maybe sub-framing will appeal to you, maybe not.
You'll only find out by experimenting. Street photography teaches
you about yourself. There are some photographers whose images
are kinetic, dynamic. They are hooked on motion and that is their
way of trying to make sense of the world. I find that approach too
noisy, it's too much to take in. I want to tidy everything up and put it
in a box within a box. Sub-framing appeals to my natural neatness;
my need to create order out of chaos.

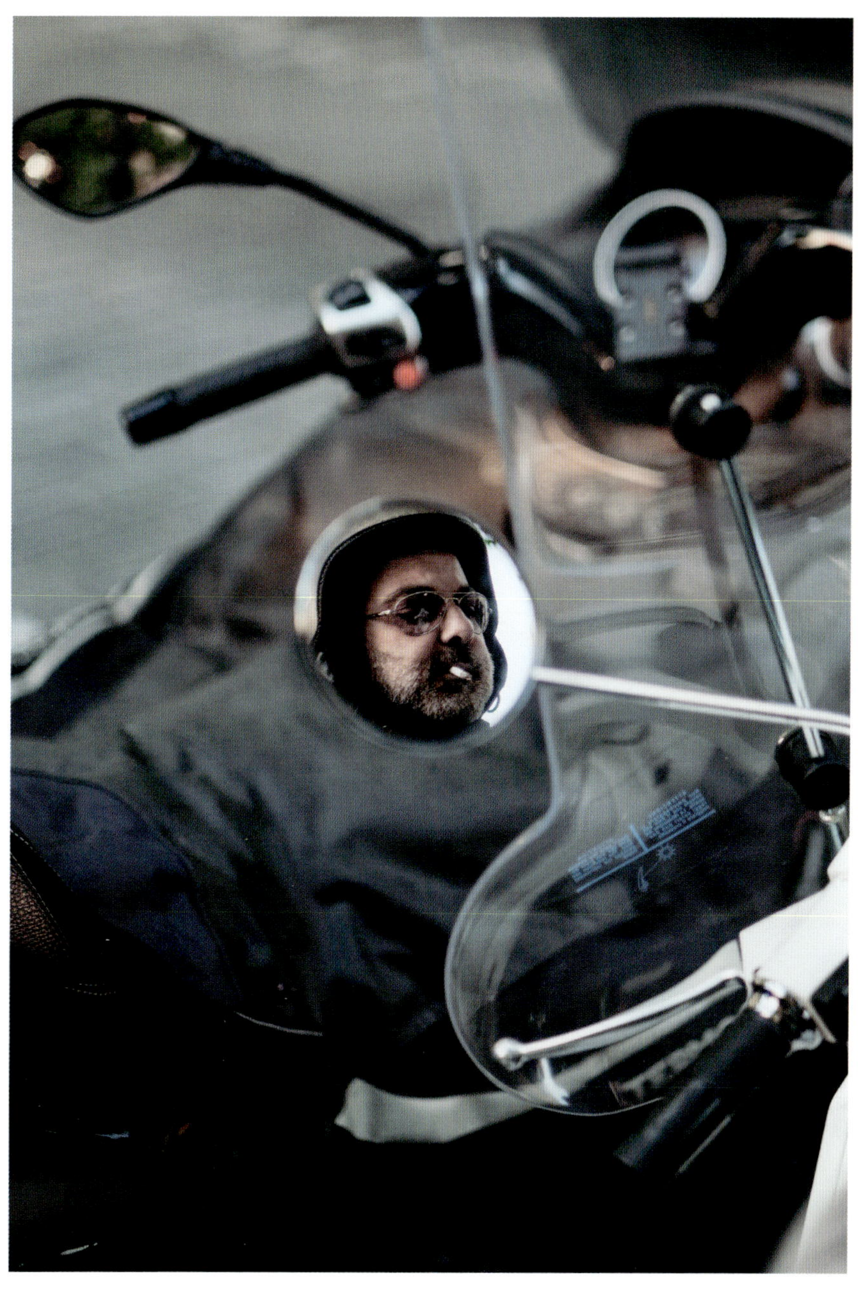

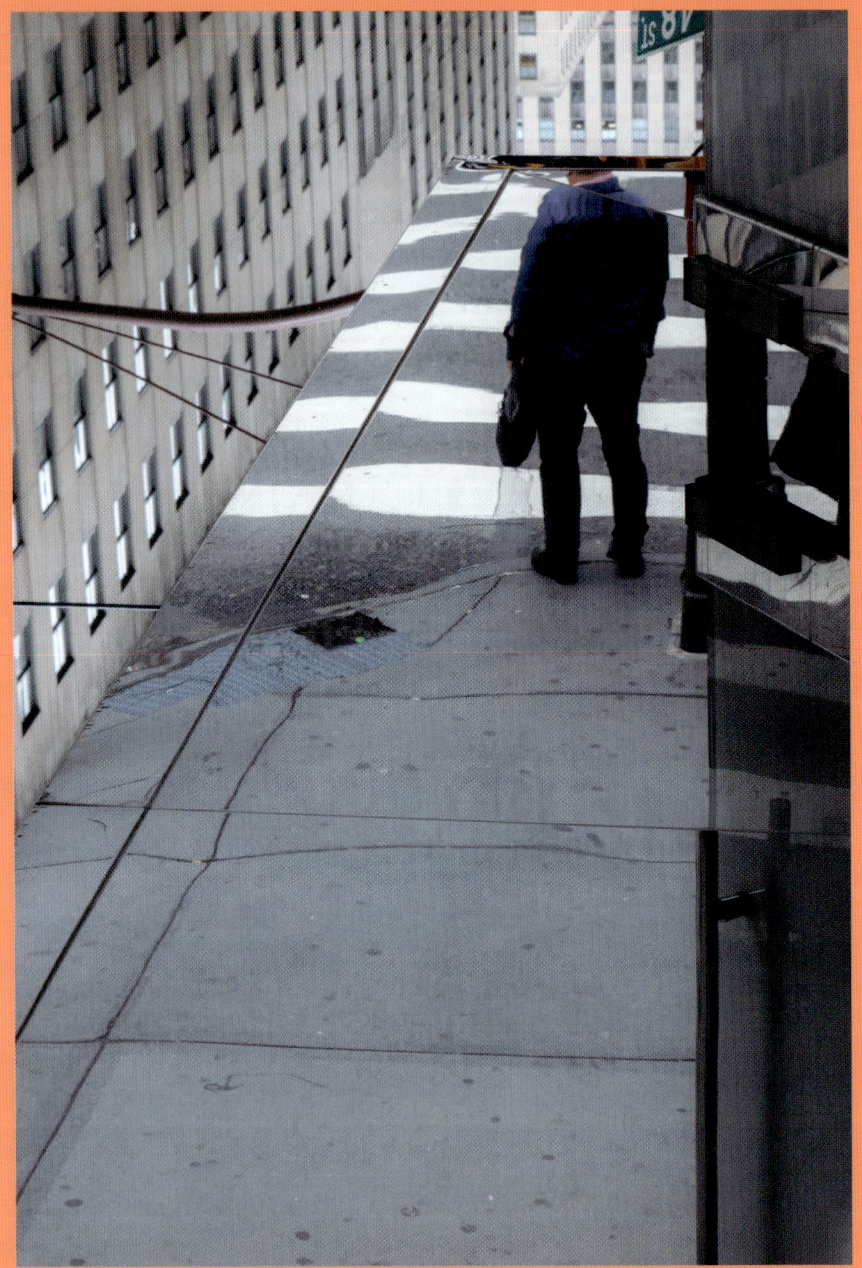

This shot resembles a collage but it's a trick of the eye, created in-camera using reflections.
New York, 2019

Mix up perspective

Make your viewers do a double-take and they will start to see the city differently

I love to be confused. What I mean when I say that, is that I like an image to keep me guessing for a while. If I can shoot something that makes people wonder how I did it, that's a mission accomplished for me. It all comes down to originality. Almost everyone has a camera these days. The cities in which we live have never been so photographed. By finding a different angle, a different perspective, you will show people something they have seen before in an original way. Perhaps, for example, you shoot something in the distance, the whole frame in focus, avoiding any of the foreground elements that help the viewer to situate it in terms of relative depth, so the image becomes flat with nothing to signify if the objects, buildings or people we are looking at are nearer or

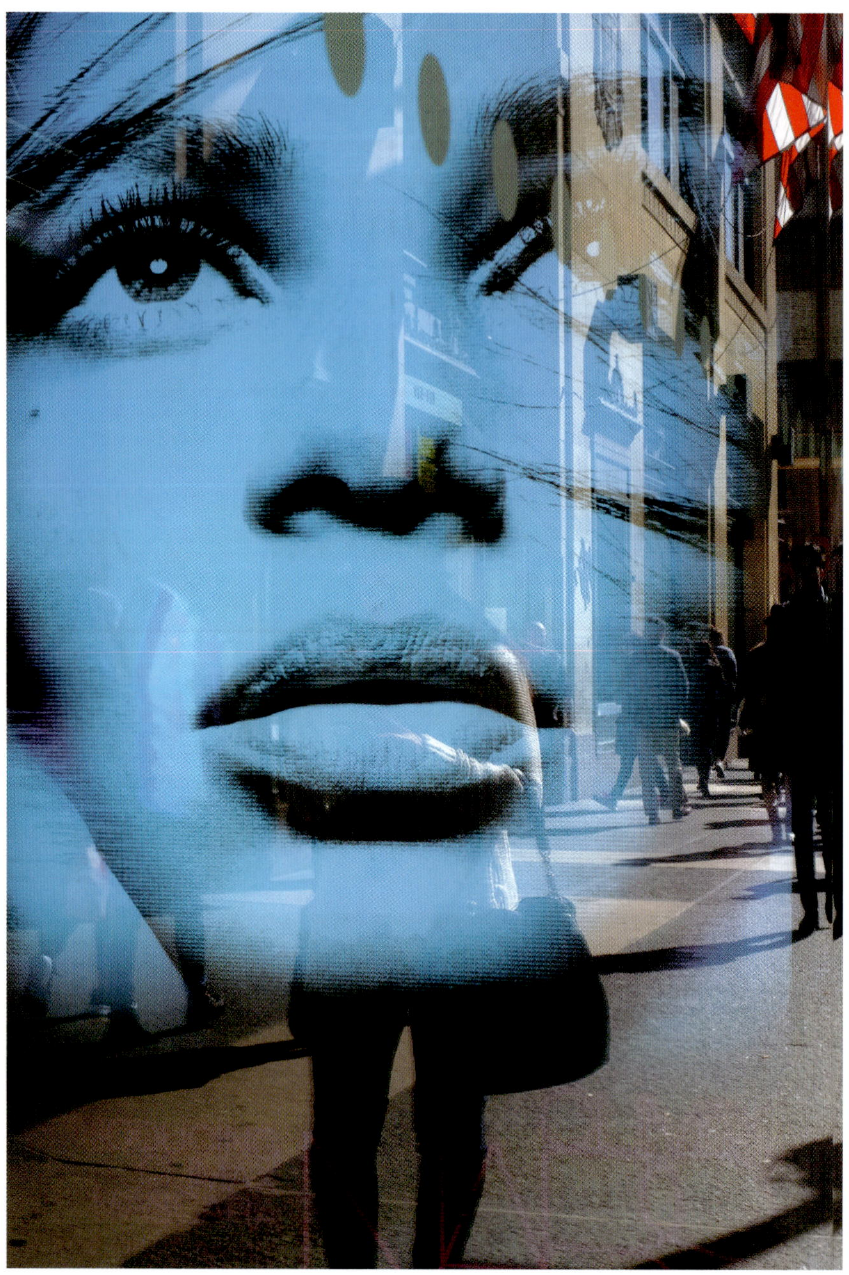

Shot through a bus stop, this image is like a visual conundrum, and that makes it compelling.
New York, 2018

further away in relation to each other. If sub-framing was about organisation, this is about confusion. Let me explain…

Fifth Avenue, New York, has been captured by street photographers for more than a century. Who knows how many photographs have been taken there, in the last week alone? When I was shooting there, I noticed the reflective overhang of an H&M store where you can see a mirror image of the pedestrians below. I decided to point my camera upwards. The resulting shot is mind-bending, a visual riddle that takes some concentration to unpack. I'm pretty sure that it has been repeated by a few other people since. Ideally, I would have preferred there to be nothing in the foreground, so that you really had no reference points. But even so, it takes a while to figure out what you're looking at. You can't see the street level but there's a lamppost. And once you get it, everything makes sense. You can flatten out the image to the point that it is impossible to dissect what is in the frame. Then, aesthetically, you have made a great abstract shot. It's beautiful because of the colours, the shapes, the composition and no one even tries to figure it out. That still has value, there's no reason not to do that. But for me, it's more interesting if you have a hint so people can enjoy the puzzle.

New York is a city of tall buildings, a place where it can pay to climb up high. Cambridge is famously flat and low architecturally. There are barely more than two storeys anywhere. What you can do, though, wherever you are, is look up. Looking down is an obvious one – we've all seen images of puddles and feet – but people don't seem to be in the habit of looking up. The same goes for looking behind you. If you're walking, you could be out shooting for a whole day, and never look back. There could be an incredible subject literally right there and you'd miss it. As the H&M example demonstrates, there are also interesting surfaces to be found above eye level. I'm more interested in the shapes of buildings above the street than their frontage. The tops of buildings also provide you with more contrast.

In another picture I made in New York, in 2020, the first two-thirds of the frame are filled with the turquoise face of a

> **'By finding a different angle, a different perspective, you will show people something they have seen before in an original way.'**

woman. It's one of the images that people message me about the most, wanting to know what they're looking at. I made it entirely in-camera by shooting against a reflection on the back of a bus stop with an illuminated advert on the inside. People often assume it must be a double exposure. They try to reverse-engineer what I've done and that's what they come up with. A really well-known image of mine, and one that many people have tried to replicate is my 'floating hat'. That one isn't just about being in the right place at the right time, it's about using the light to create a surreal illusion. At certain times of the year, the light in the Lion Yard Shopping Centre in Cambridge comes in through a roof with a lattice pattern, creating diamond-shaped spots of light on the floor. The exit in the distance leads on to a street that is in full shadow, so you end up with what is essentially a frame with a dark backdrop and spotlighting. Then you just need the right subject and the invisible man appears.

There is a photographer from Barcelona called Pau Buscató whose method is really grounded in juxtaposition. He has a shot that I'll never forget. It shows a building site in London. Four birds in flight are printed on the construction hoarding. Your eye follows their line to see a bird-shaped rip in some white netting and, just above the rip is a real pigeon flying past. What you see at first glance is six birds in flight. It's one of those images you stare at before you realise what you're actually seeing. At first, I thought, 'That's cool'. Then, 'That can't be real.' Then I got it. That kind of image goes down well on social media because it stops people for a minute. But it can also work in a gallery space or a book. Any time you can stop someone flicking through the pages or walking around the room and take a bit more time to look at something, you've won.

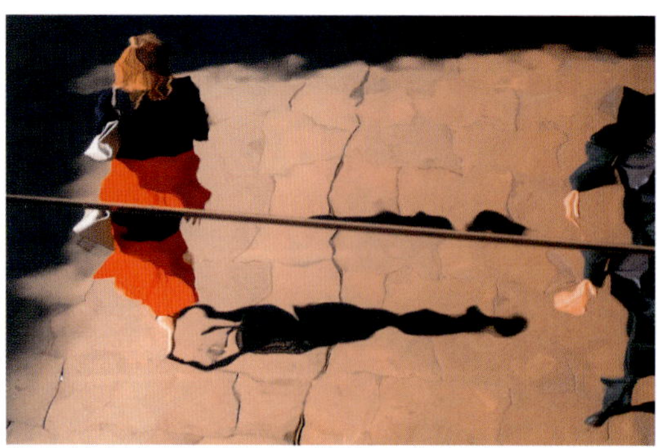

Light can create natural distortions, from water-like ripple effects to the illusion of invisibility.

RIGHT
London, 2018

LEFT
Cambridge, 2017

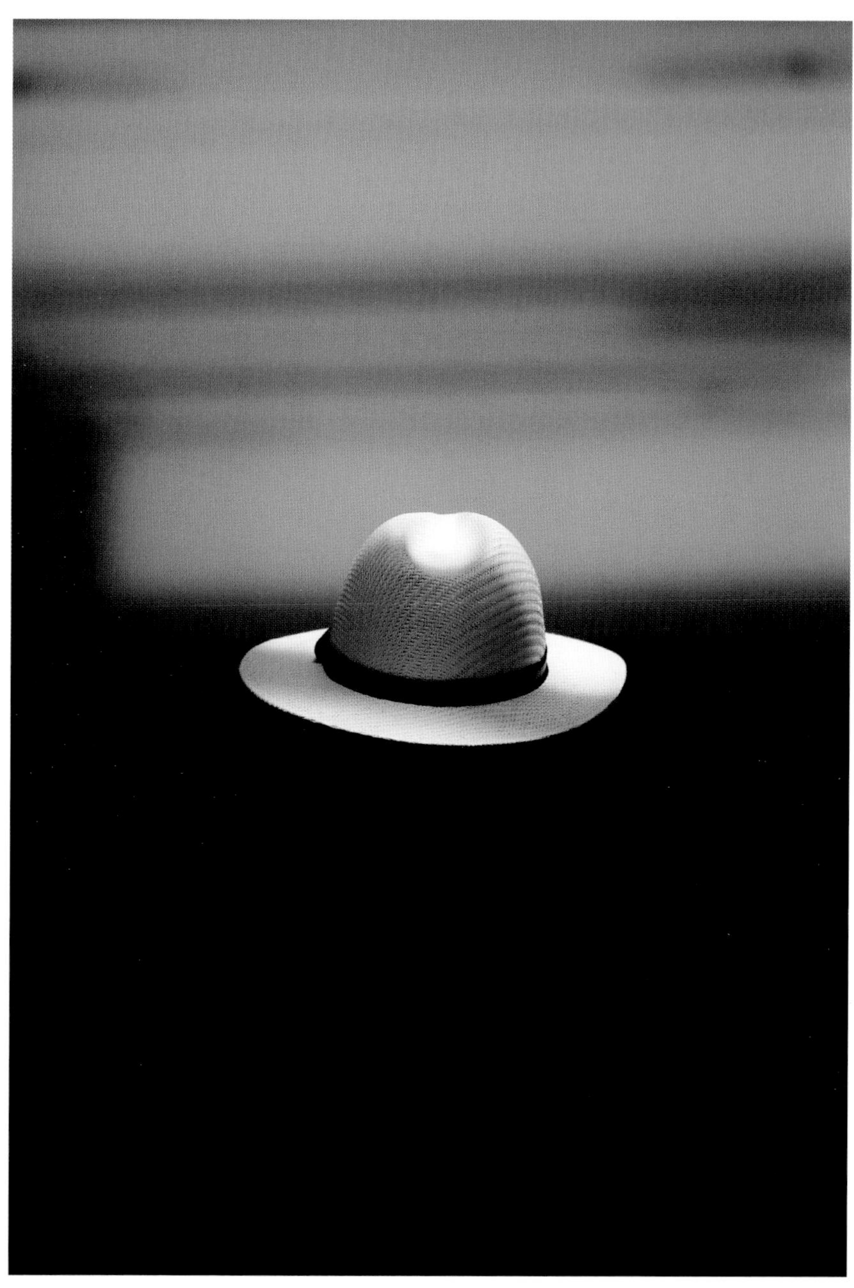

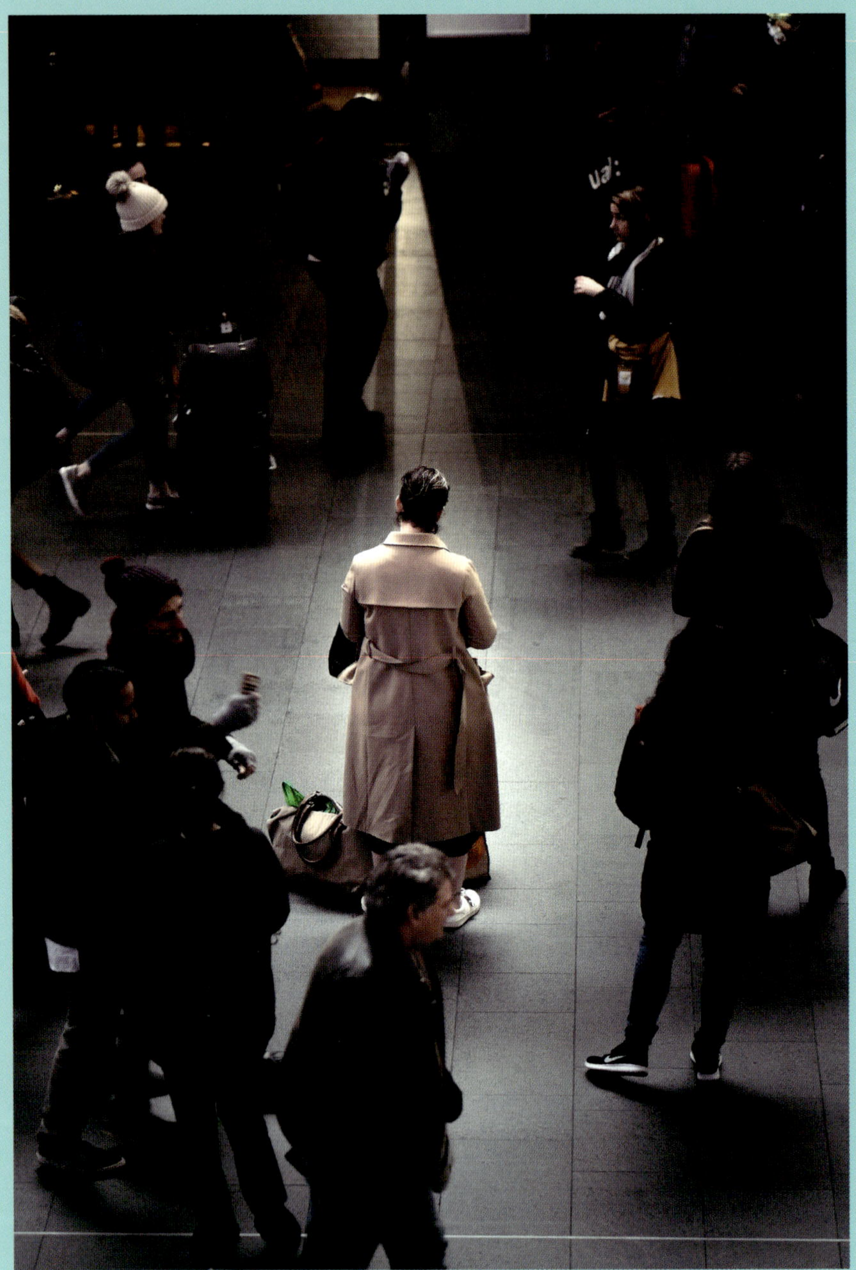

This shaft of illumination created a natural spotlight. I had to capture its theatrical effect.
London, 2017

14

Follow the light

Allow yourself to be led by the light – it's what makes your images come alive

The word 'photography' translates from Greek as 'drawing with light' and this lies at the root of everything I do. Light is, without fail, the very first thing I think about – before leading lines, contrast, sub-framing, perspective, and certainly before people – and it completely determines my schedule. The most remarkable moment on the street is insignificant if the lighting doesn't do it justice. In fact, my photography heroes – Saul Leiter and Ernst Haas – aren't noted for the remarkable moments they captured but for their painterly approach to light and colour.

Leiter was an absolute magician with the light. Many of my favourite shots of his weren't taken on sunny days, but on rainy, snowy, cold days where condensation covers the windows. Equally impactful, in 1955 Haas took an extraordinary photograph, in portrait orientation, of the side of an epic New York skyscraper, its gigantic steel form glinting in the sunlight. The rectangular shadows

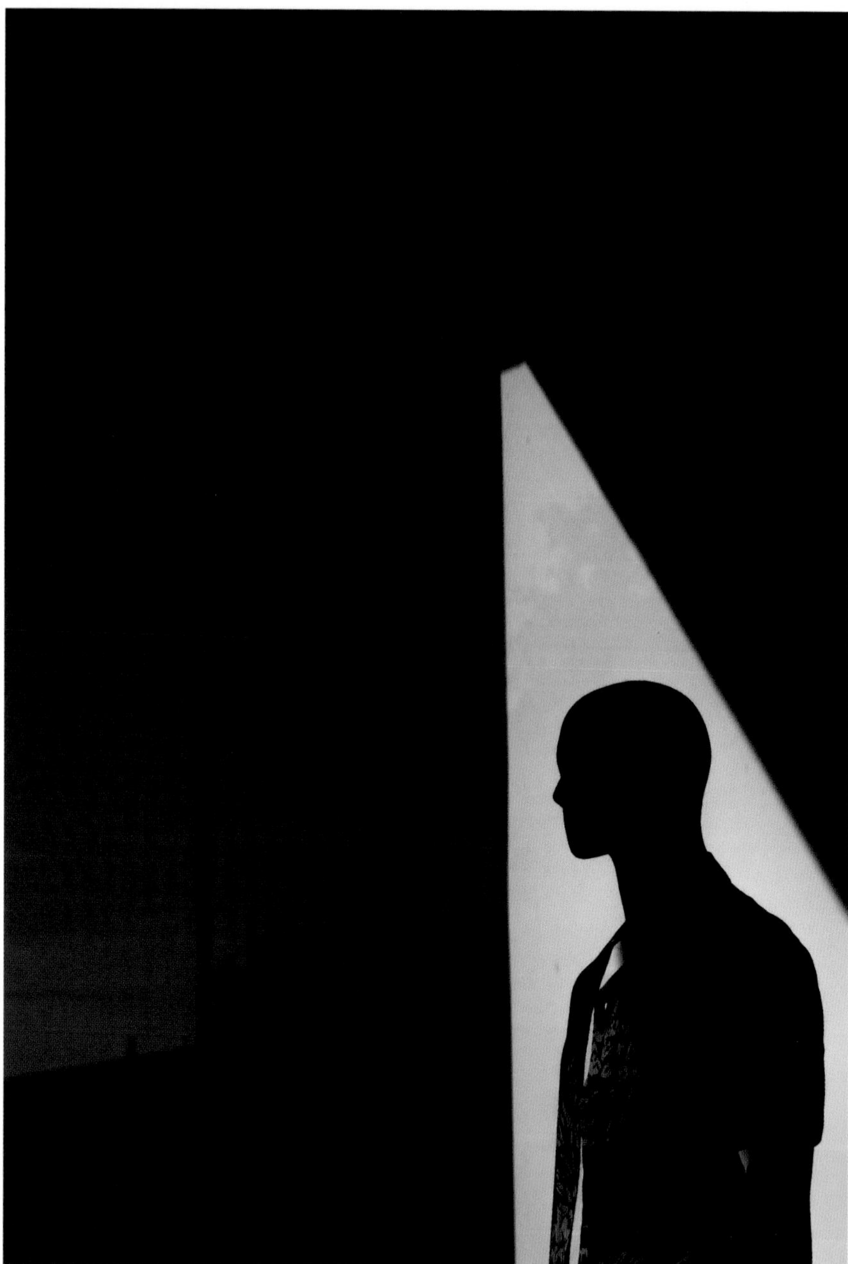

My optimal light is the strong, harsh kind that gives rise to bold compositions like this.
Cambridge, 2020

of other buildings act like steps, leading you down from the top of the skyscraper to the bottom of the frame and the single red circle of a traffic light. Everything in the image pulls you towards that red light. Haas was a genius for noticing that it was the light that made the composition. I often wonder when he'd spotted it. Maybe he realised a week prior, but the sun's position wasn't quite right or perhaps he spotted it as it was and was really that lucky, who knows?

'The most remarkable moment on the street is insignificant if the lighting doesn't do it justice.'

The best times of day to shoot are in the evening or the morning. That's when shadows cut across windows or buildings, giving you strong shapes to work with. I prefer to shoot first thing in the morning. You see interesting things and different people that you'd miss at other times of day. Also, as I started shooting around a day job, it allowed me to be more productive, to learn about the light and to know what scenes would be well lit. I would move around the city, paying attention to how the light struck certain spots, and thinking about how that would change so that I could revisit them at different times. Sometimes, if I don't get the shot I'm after, I might wait six months for the light to come back to the spot from a different angle and try again. Until I get that gut feeling that says, 'That's the one,' I'm not going to settle for anything less.

I'm always on the hunt for a strong light source that will make everything in the frame pop. This doesn't have to be the sun. Shooting at night, I look for artificial light sources I can use, from shops, streetlamps flashing adverts and neon signs to moving vehicles such as police cars and ambulances. The more temporary a light source, the better, because that allows you to capture something that will never be repeated. I like the colours in my images to be really saturated and I'm conscious of how different hues respond to one another. Most of all, I'm drawn to primary colours. As much as the American flag is a political symbol, I just love the combination of red, white and blue. You see it in so many images by the old masters of street photography. You can see why it has become such a powerful icon.

In Cambridge, there used to be a hotel called The University Arms. In 2015, some of the building was demolished so that it could be redeveloped. I took many pictures during the construction work, including one of a man in a striped hoodie walking past some striped hoarding (shown on cover). It was a pivotal picture that helped bring me to the attention of a bigger audience. With the new building complete, each year in September at the right time of day, the light comes straight through a certain window and hits the concierge's desk. I tend to hang around outside the main doors, waiting for people to come in and out. Whenever the doors open, you get this great composition that's defined by the shape of the window with the light pouring through it. I was shooting there in 2018, and someone opened the door to the luggage store at the same time. Suddenly, a bright-red suitcase in the store produced this incredible, unpredictable flash of vibrant colour that was very specific to that time and that day.

Red features a lot in my work, probably more than any other colour. The old colour masters I admire most likely shot on Kodachrome film and the reds, blues and yellows in my work are all kind of skewed towards the colour that that film produced. This, paired with the fact that painting and illustration were my first influences, means I find myself trying to recreate those bold colours in clean compositions. That's why I seek strong light, which makes every shade look more vibrant. I'm influenced as much by the colours I don't like as the ones that I do. I can't stand the fluorescent yellow of a high vis jacket. My yellows are always tinged with mustard or more orange in tone. If that is something I can fix in the edit, I absolutely will. My reaction to colours is quite visceral. There have been times when I've seen a potential picture but thought, 'I hate that colour,' and I just won't take it. I used to only ever shoot in colour, but I'm being a little less strict with myself these days. Now, if the light is right, I'm happy to shoot in black and white for the sake of a brilliant composition. Sometimes the only thing to do is bend the rules.

'The more temporary a light source, the better, because that allows you to capture something that will never be repeated.'

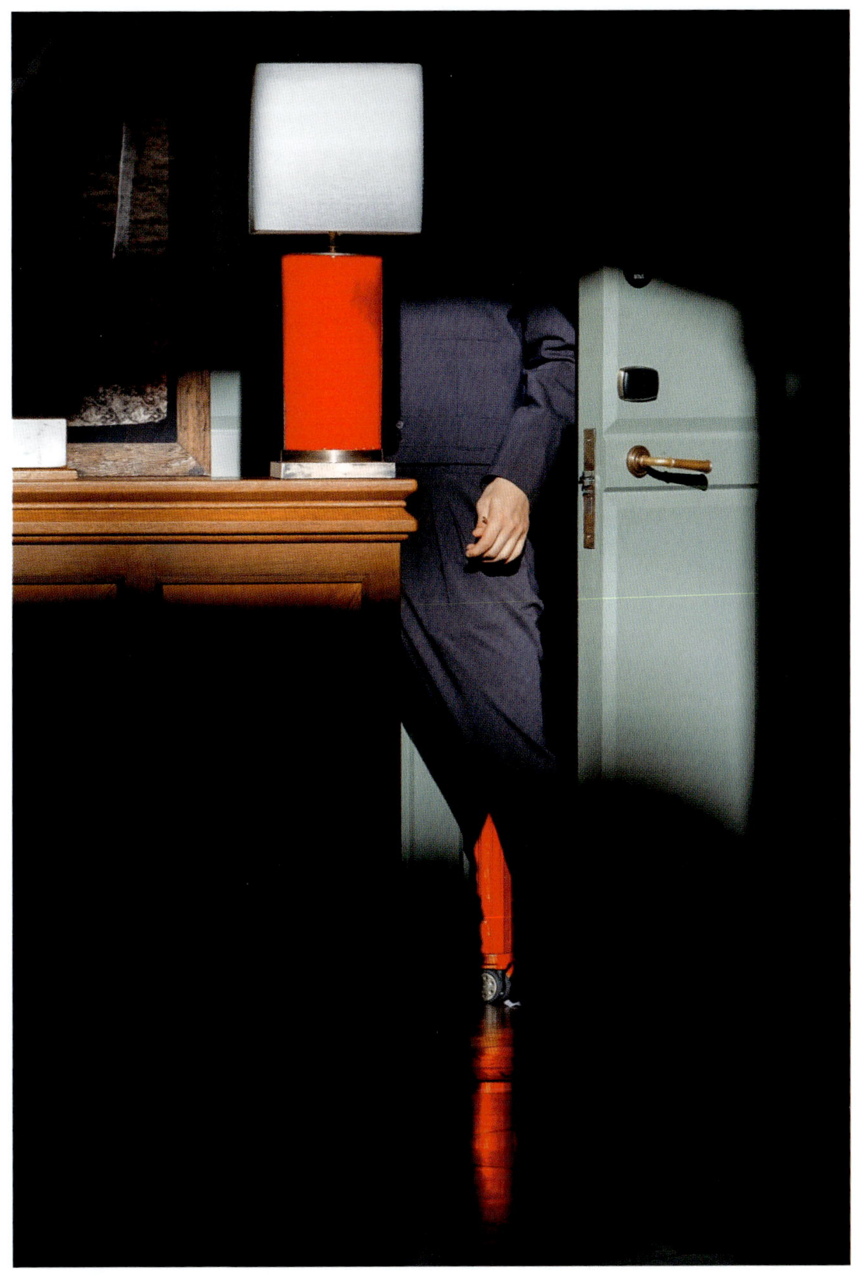

Light changes so much throughout the day and season. This shot was a real one-off.
Cambridge, 2018

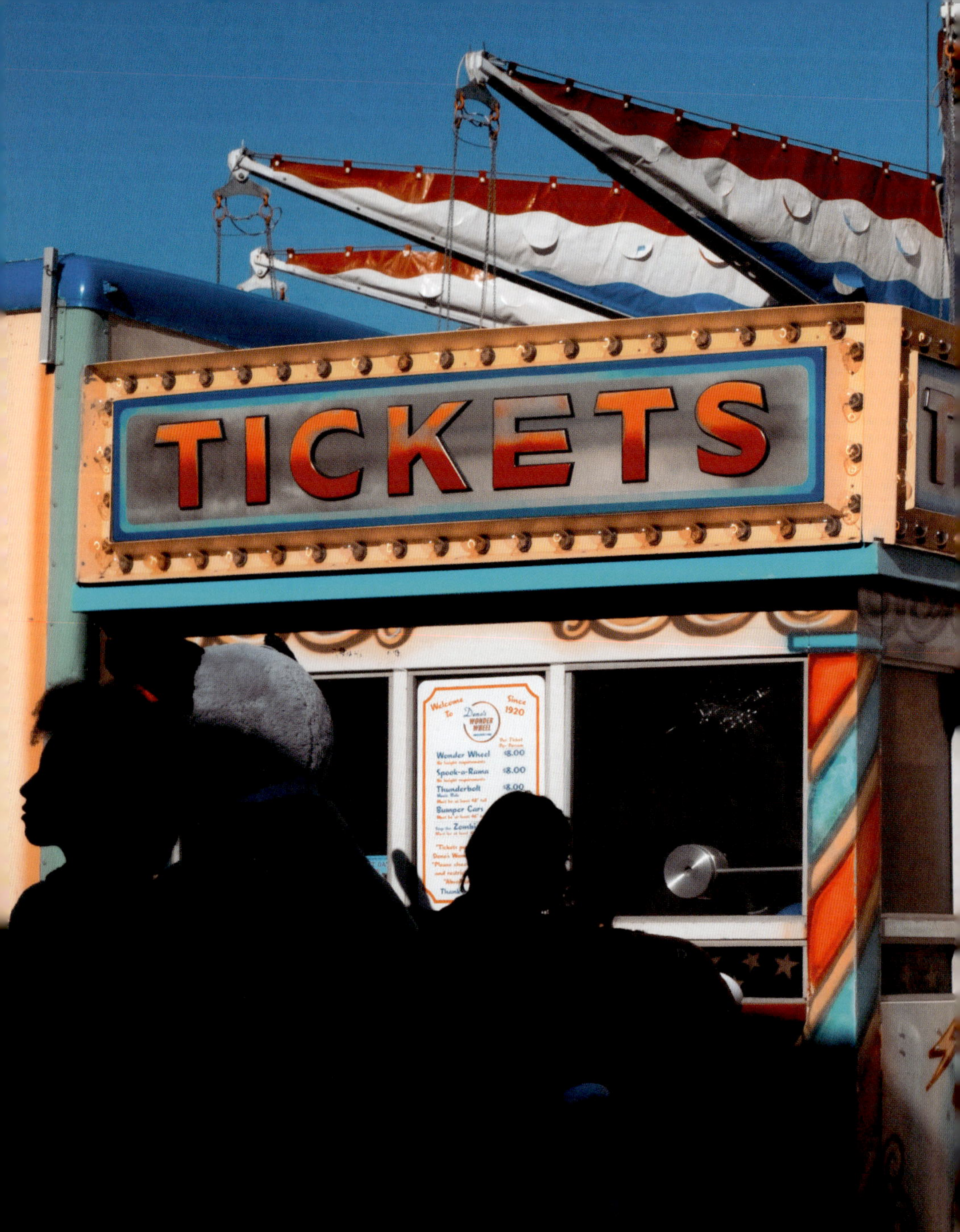

TICKETS
Welcome To Deno's WONDER WHEEL Since 1920
One Ticket Per Person
Wonder Wheel $8.00
Spook-a-Rama $8.00
Thunderbolt $8.00
Bumper Cars
Zombie

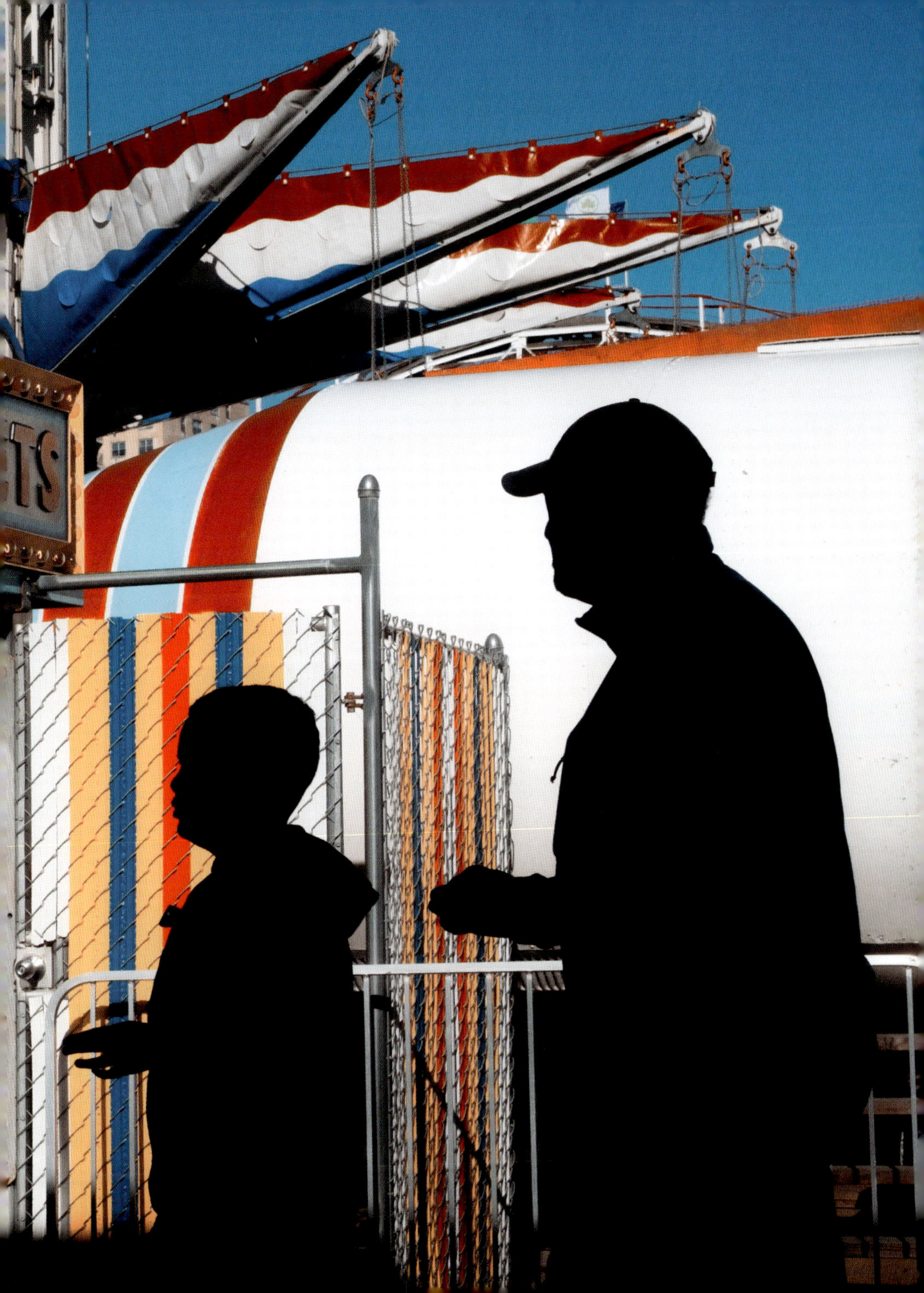
TS

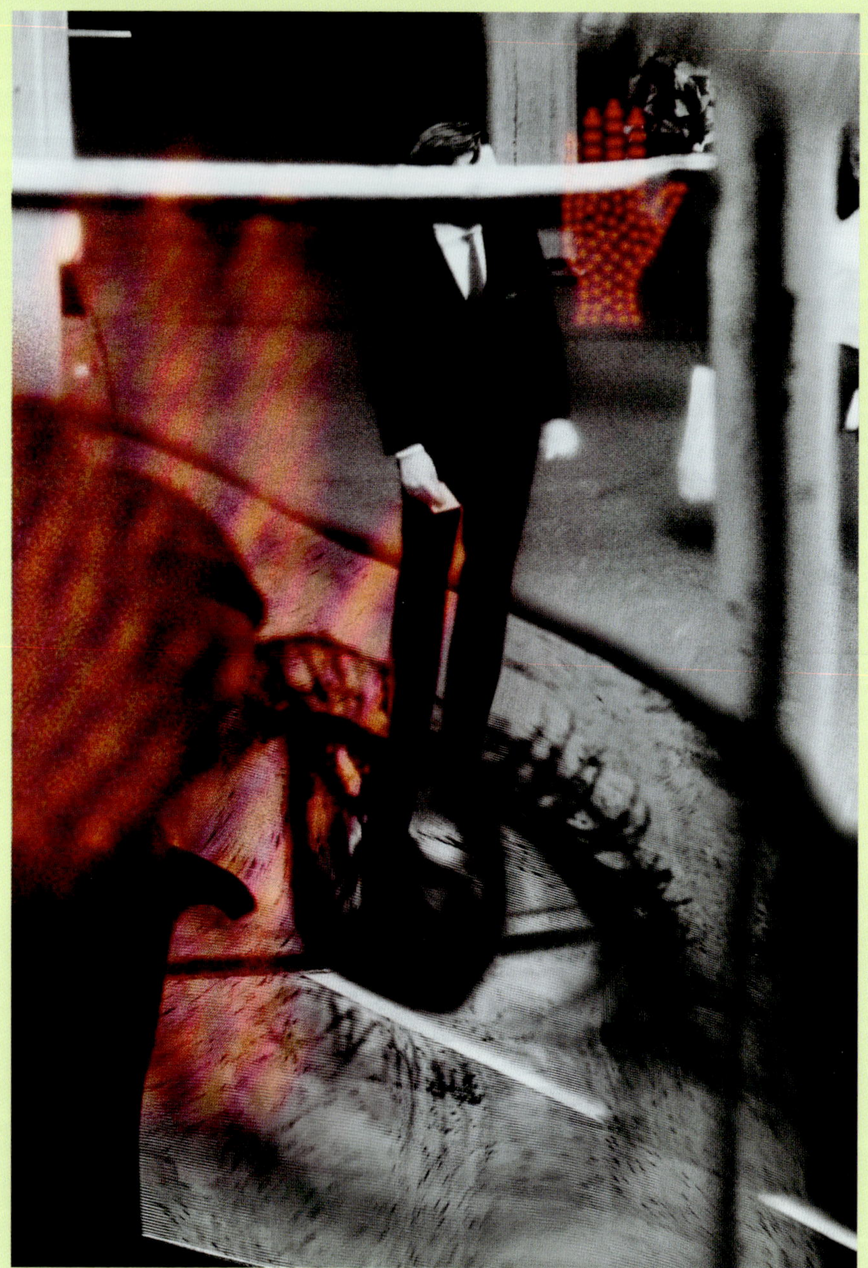

Pictures like this one combine figurative elements – the eyes, the person – in an abstract way.
New York, 2022

15

Abstract the world

Learn to see the reflection before you see what's beyond it

There comes a point when your eye is so attuned to looking at the world photographically that you can't remember how it looked before. I realise this every time I come across a window. Of course, the whole purpose of a window is to allow light to enter a building – and to let people see in and out. But to me a window is a surface. When I look at that sheet of glass, I see the reflections in it rather than the person on the other side. This has given rise to awkward situations. I'll be pointing my camera right at some beautiful interplay of colours on glass when I suddenly see someone looking straight through with a slightly surprised look on their face. This happens more often than I'd like to admit. But in the main, my abstracted way of looking serves me well.

My pictures are never purely abstract rather I use elements of abstraction by photographing people against the light to create

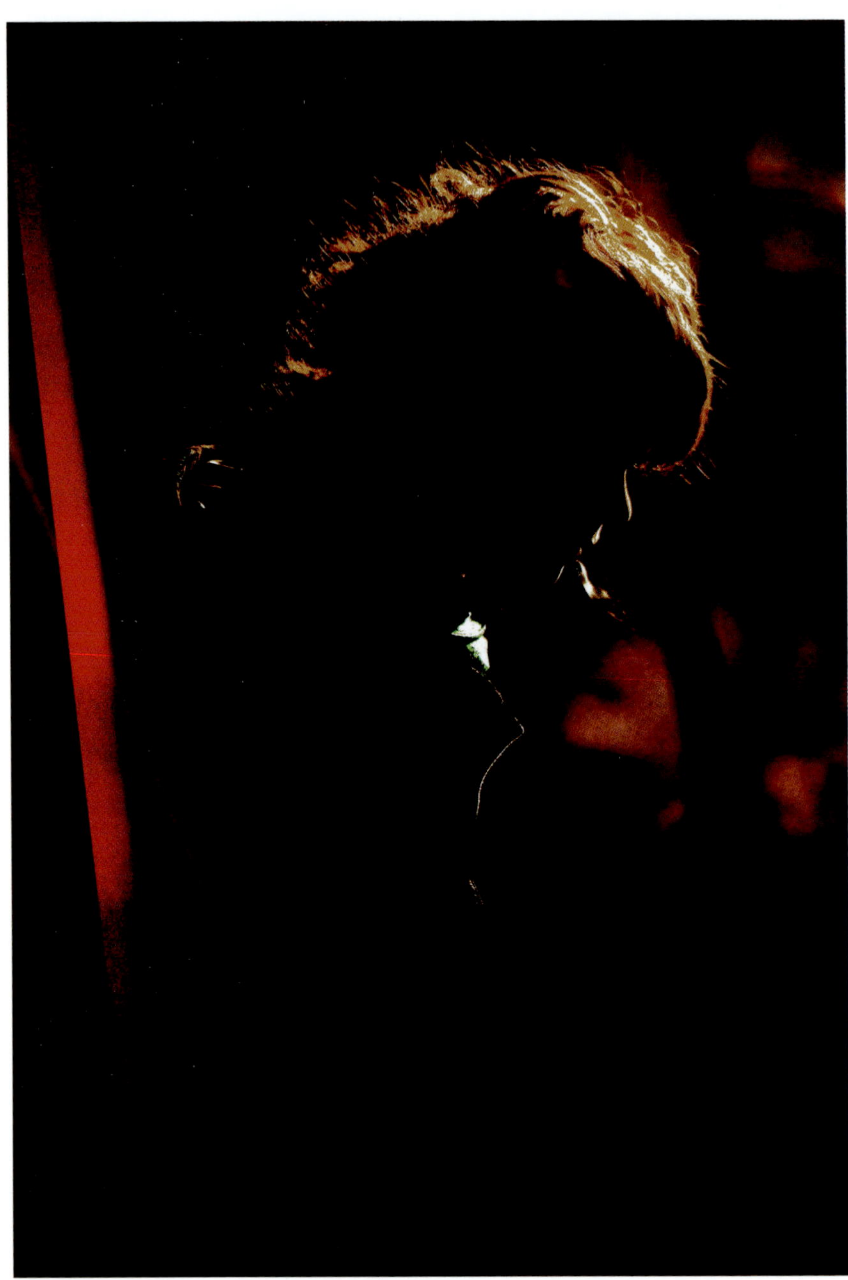

Silhouettes are a constant in my work. I'm drawn to shapes, rather than facial expressions.
ABOVE Cambridge, 2022
RIGHT London, 2018

silhouettes that mean they're more like shapes than characters, for example. Faces interest me less than gestures, colours, lines, form and texture. I love shooting through things like reeded glass, for example, which gives an image a kind of rippled, almost corrugated style. That takes away the 'story' element and for me, makes it more complicated and more interesting. It's too simple just to take a photograph of the thing right in front of you. That's what everyone else is doing. Make it harder for yourself, add layers in there. It's an extra challenge, sure, but it's also more fun.

I have a mental bank of objects to shoot through, just like I have a mental bank of locations or light situations around a city that I return to again and again. I might see a window or glass doorway with warped glass at an hour of day when there's no one around. Next time I'm walking down the same street, I'll check, and maybe stop, in case someone shows up on the other side. I once took a picture through a really scratched perspex panel in a bus stop. If it had been all nicely refurbished, the photo wouldn't have worked because the scratches give it an atmosphere. You can hardly see through it, so when there's strong light early in the day and early in the year, something extraordinary happens. In my image, it's misty almost, with everything seeped in red and just the top of the subject's hair and her profile lit up. You can use your camera settings to create abstracted effects, too, working a slow shutter speed to blur action like here, so the whole scene melts into colour and shape and only a human silhouette anchors it in reality.

'It's too simple just to take a photograph of the thing right in front of you. That's what everyone else is doing.'

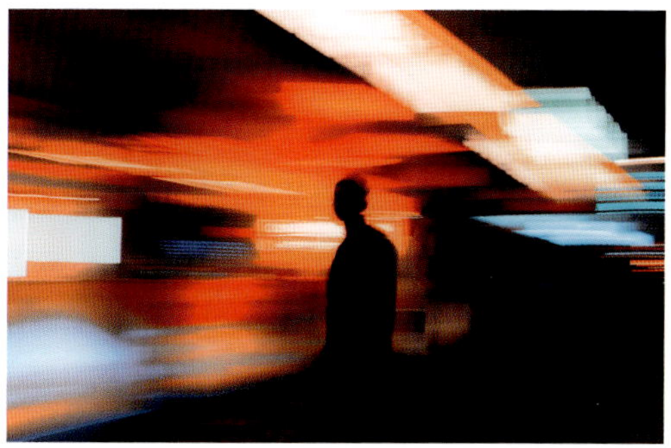

Bus windows on rainy days are classic for creating smudgy, semi-abstract scenes, but as the old buses get replaced, such images are harder to make because new buses have windows that don't steam up. I have a few shots of condensation-covered café windows where you can just make out a hand pushed against them, but these are all disappearing too, with refits and refurbishments. It's one of those everyday sights we might one day look back on as a relic from another era, and that makes them all the more interesting to document now. I'm also always looking to fill a frame with repetition – patterns made by steps or columns or a collection of people, for example. A solitary person is rarely remarkable. But 10 or 20 people all dressed in the same colour clothing, like the troupe of men in suits all in step, holding blue and white striped umbrellas (see page 48) or a crowd of people all coincidentally eating ice creams at the same time, can make a great picture.

There's also something about anonymity in abstraction that makes an image universal in ways that are harder to achieve otherwise. The people in any given shot are what gives it a narrative. If it's too specific – say it's based only on what a person happens to be wearing, what they look like or their face – it's boring, but if there's something happening that could be applied to anyone, a really compelling moment, emotionally, that's interesting. Perceiving the world in this way is a little like London cabbies doing 'the Knowledge' – the test in which they must learn every main road, side street and alleyway in the UK capital by heart. An exercise like that rewires your brain in ways that can never really be reversed.

'There's something about anonymity in abstraction that makes an image universal in ways that are harder to achieve otherwise.'

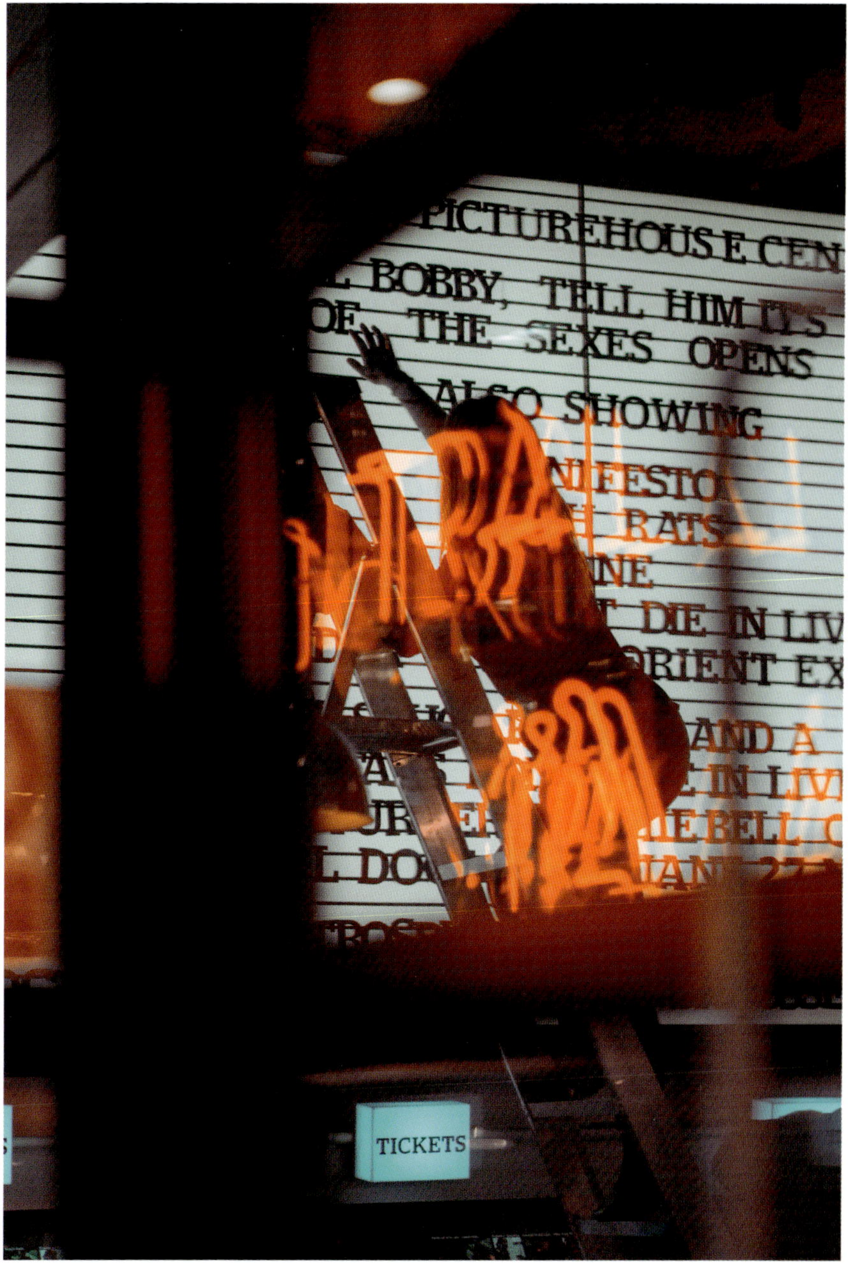

By subtracting the specifics of an individual, you open up an image to multiple interpretations.
London, 2017

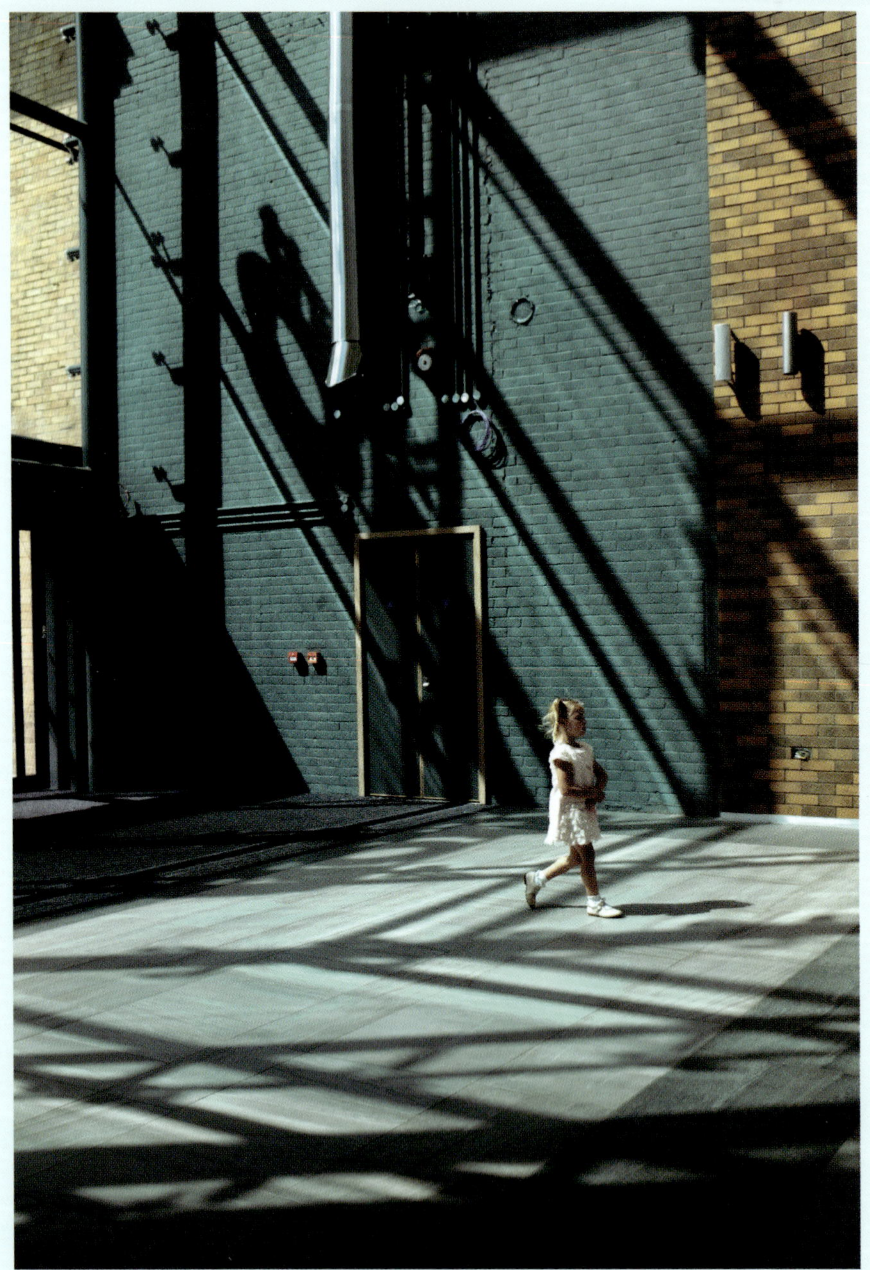

Cambridge is a city steeped in history but that's not what you take away from my images.
Cambridge, 2017

16

Know your patch

Compile a mental library of locations across your city that you can return to time and again

Think street photography, and you think of New York, a city of towering skyscrapers, yellow taxis, home to more than eight million people. You don't think of Cambridge – a historic town in England known for its prestigious university and pretty buildings, with a population of less than 150,000. There's no wonder the Big Apple is synonymous with the genre. It's where many of the greats cut their teeth, including the photographers who have influenced me the most – Saul Leiter and Ernst Haas. There is a whole set of picture postcard images that come to mind when you think of Cambridge – the backs of the colleges, cyclists, students in gowns – and I've avoided it consistently.

I've never been a fan of the architecture and never really paid attention to the things that make it unique, like the porters who work at the colleges of the university, but every now and then I might take a picture of one of them and they are always popular

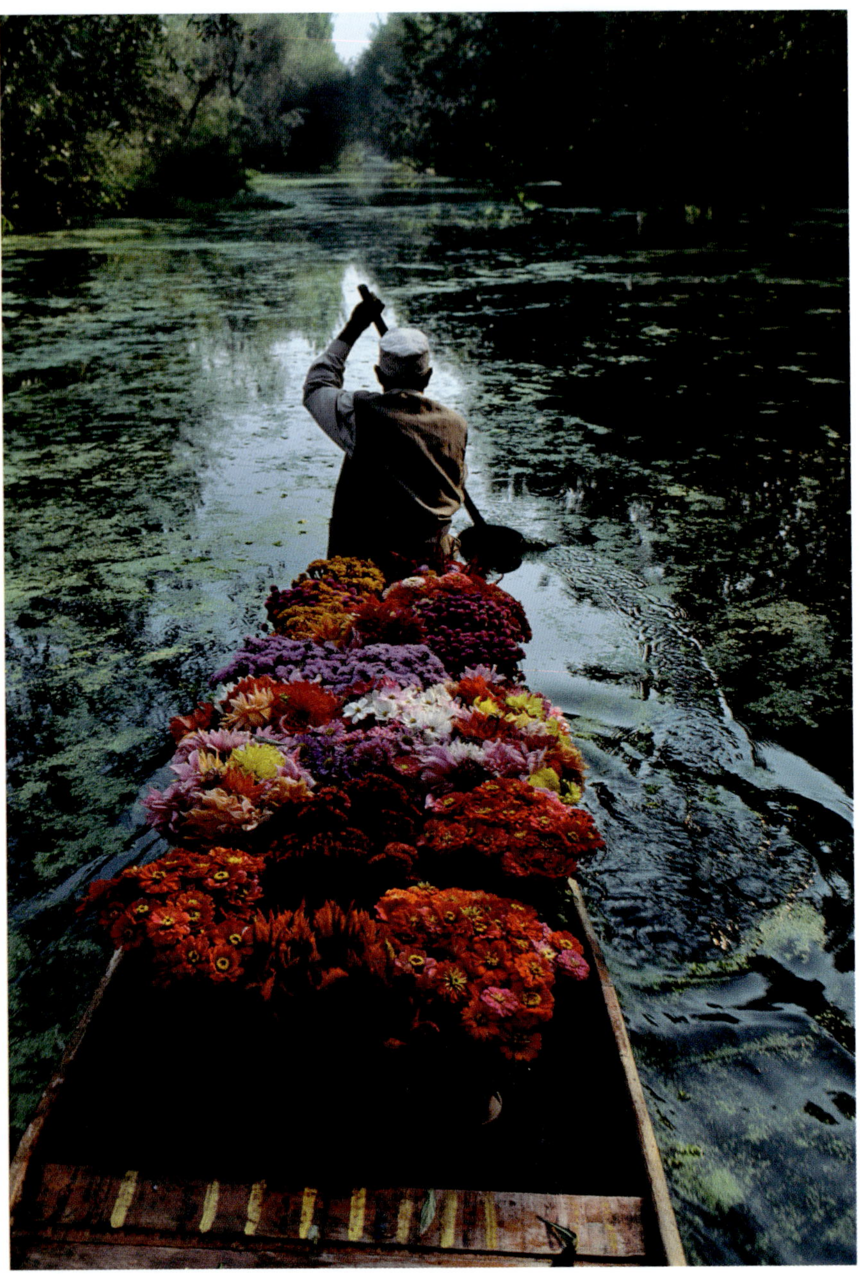

I've been trying to capture a shot inspired by this on the River Cam. It's only a matter of time.
© Steve McCurry / Magnum Photos

on social media. It makes sense because this is something I see every day, but most people don't ever get to see it. Sometimes I think I need to stop rejecting it simply because it's not the aesthetic that I have in my mind. But it feels too touristy. Anything too obviously 'nice' just doesn't draw me in. I think, 'Well, if anyone else had walked down this road at this precise moment with a camera in their hand, that is exactly the shot they would have taken. So, what's the point?' It would be different if I saw a composition that others might come up with, but that featured an environment that they don't have access to, and so it doesn't exist already. *Then*, I might take the shot.

I'll give you an example – a shot I've been trying to get for some time. The scene reminds me of a 1999 image by Magnum photographer Steve McCurry where you see a man from behind using a pole to paddle a boat that is piled high with red, purple, yellow and white flowers through Dal Lake, in India. The context is different, of course, but there's something about it that sparks a similarity. The shot I want to get shows a punter going under the Mathematical Bridge in Queens' College. Built in 1749, the bridge is based on an ingenious design by James King that uses gravity to keep all the elements in suspension. Very Cambridge! There's a building on the right-hand side and the trees are full of leaves because it's summer, and the intersection between those two things creates a perfect triangle in the water – just like the McCurry image. And in the sky, there is another big, bright V shape. These shapes are right at the apex of the setting pole which is used to move the punt along. You have to go there early in the morning to get the right light, and at the weekend, otherwise there's no one out on the River Cam.

Sometimes you need to travel, to expand your horizons a little, to realise what makes the place you're from special. If you can't do that for whatever reason, you can still be exposed to all the different countries and cities in the world through the internet. That is one of the great advantages of social media – you can easily see where everyone else is shooting street photography and get some understanding of it from that. Ultimately, it all comes down to the old idea of showing people familiar things in a new way – or new things in a familiar way. If you're photographing something no one's ever seen before, you don't need to do something unheard of with the way you capture it. Conversely, really creative portrait photography works because it takes a face, something you spend your entire life looking at, and reveals it to you it in a way you've never seen before.

Knowing your patch is about understanding what is distinctive about the place where you live or shoot, and appreciating its own pros and cons for street photography. It's also about knowing the streets back to front. This only comes from the hours you put in, walking around, observing from every angle, at all times of day and season. I remember, as a rollerblade-mad kid, sitting in the car on journeys with my parents, staring out of the window at the city as it passed, like it was a movie. I'd see a rail and think, I need to remember where that is, I want to come back and skate that. I was constantly alert and it's the same now, only I'm looking for images.

I keep a mental bank of locations, scenes, objects and light sources from the city around me. Mostly I'll hold on to these for a few days, but some I'll keep for longer. There was a spot in New York I kept in mind for a year. On my first visit, I passed a certain wall at the wrong time of day and didn't have a chance to revisit it at precisely the right time for another year. It was clichéd and well known, but something I had to tick off mentally. These things aren't stored systematically in spreadsheets and folders somewhere on my laptop – they're in my head or on my camera. Earlier, I talked about the importance of taking lots of pictures. This is a brilliant way to loosen up creatively, but it's also a way of making notes. I might never look at these 'test shots' properly again, but the act of lifting up my camera and recording a particular location as a potential composition helps cement it in my memory.

Much of what is held in the 'bank' is temporary because the city is always on the move, always changing. I tend to spot something and think, 'That's quite a nice frame, I'll come back to that tomorrow or next week, try that one again. In January 2019, I spotted how the midday winter light strikes the steps of the Ivy in Cambridge and, after several visits, I got this shot of someone entering the restaurant in red high-heeled shoes. But generally, I don't hold on to things for too long. There have only been a few occasions where I've really obsessed about one thing and had to keep going back until I got a shot. The punt is like that for me now. I'll get there in the end.

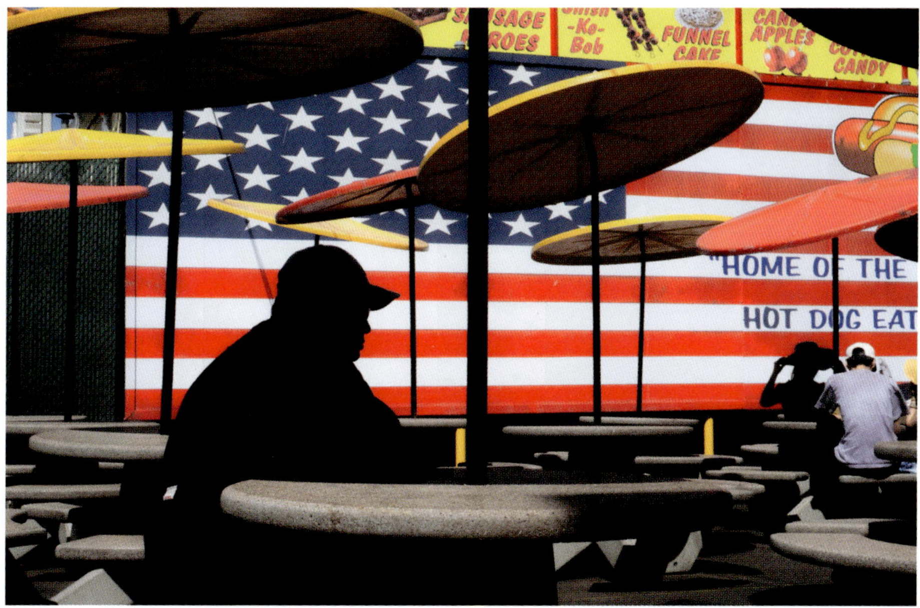

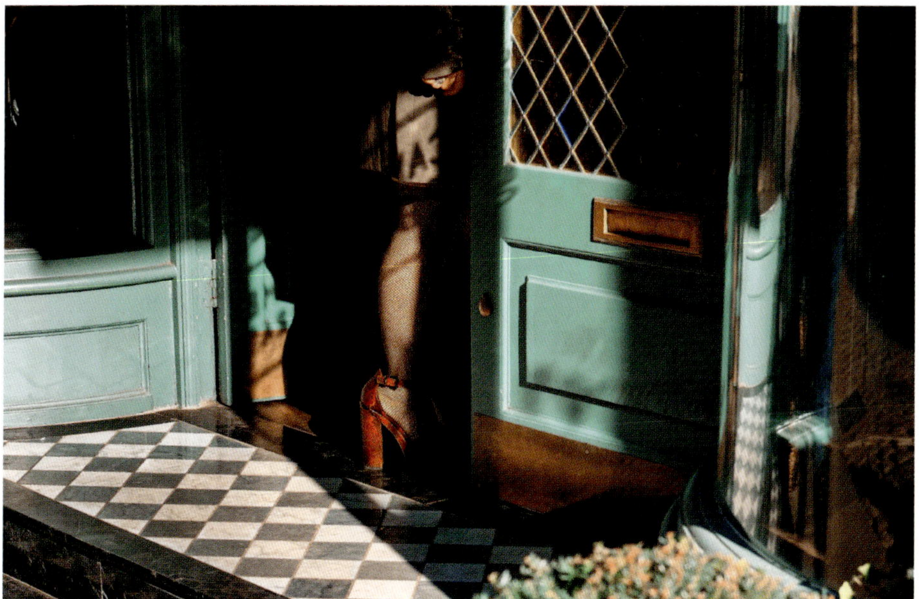

I have a mental library of spots I'd like to photograph – in ways that avoid the obvious.
ABOVE New York, 2019
BELOW Cambridge, 2019

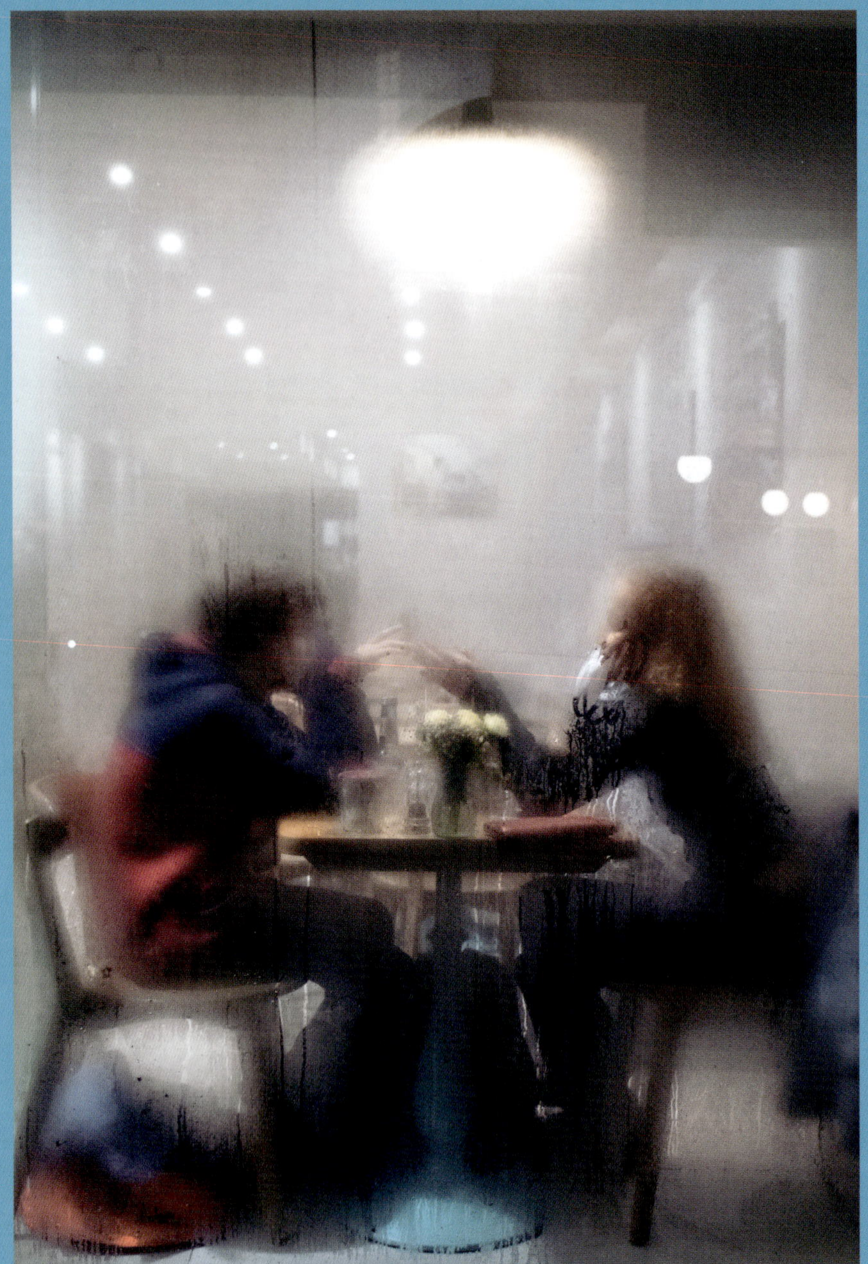

Wait before you edit. This will give you the breathing space to see what's really worth keeping.
Cambridge, 2017

17

Be a sharp critic

Create a distance from your images so you can be objective when selecting them

I don't hold back when it comes to taking pictures. At the end of a week away shooting in a foreign city, I can easily have accumulated 10,000 images, including test shots, although on a lunchtime wander around Cambridge, I might just take a handful. Say I come back with 50 shots from a day out shooting; they will likely be focused on two or three things I thought were interesting. As I look back at them, I might decide one of them actually wasn't all that good and then some might be missing an extra element I wanted to capture. So, I might only import eight photos – the ones that I look back at and think about editing.

Where possible, I always leave time between shooting and editing, the longer the better. It helps me to be less emotionally invested. When I'm going through my images, I'll usually have one of the frames open as I'm editing it, but I'll simultaneously be scrolling through the other, often almost identical, versions. If I really

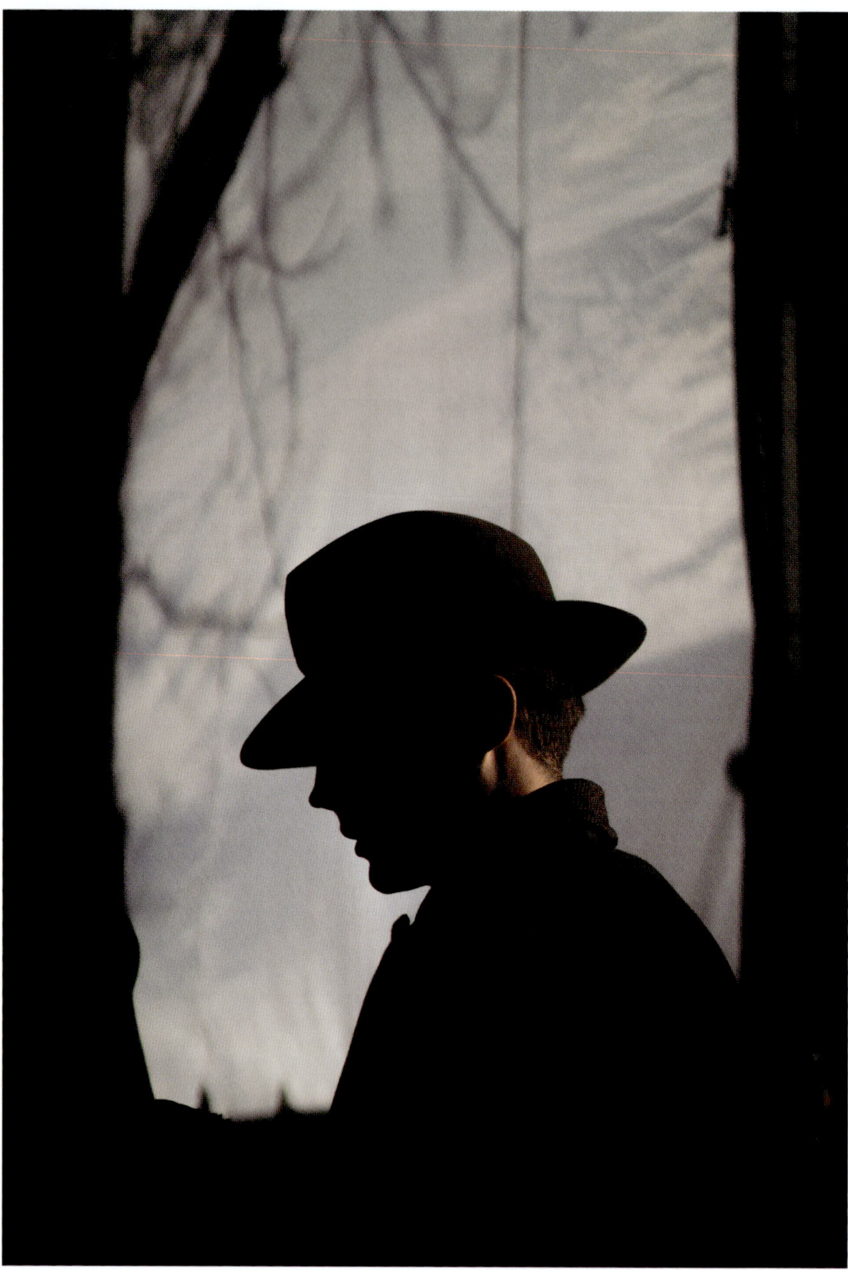

To make the cut, an image needs to be like this, bold enough to grab me even as a thumbnail.
Cambridge, 2017

can't decide between them, I'll just stare at the smaller 'navigator' version. Because composition is such an important aspect of my photography, if an image doesn't grab my attention when it's tiny, for me that means it's too busy. Normally, with a choice between four or five frames, I'll have a good idea as to which one of them is going to be stronger. When I'm choosing between two, a quick back and forth will do it.

I don't tend to share my work until I've made my own selection. If I'm shooting with someone, and we're capturing the same thing but from different angles, there's a good chance we'd compare what we'd got on the back of our cameras. And then you get a good idea of whose shot is better. If they get the best version of that shot, I'll move on to something else. More generally, I make a point of looking at other street photographers' work as much as possible. Some people avoid that because it makes them feel bad and worry that they'll never compete, but I find it motivating. I'll get annoyed if I feel my work isn't as good and push myself to their level.

'Some small element might jump out that passed you by initially because your concentration was elsewhere.'

I rely heavily on my phone to find original files. I have everything accessible there. You learn as much, if not more, from the images you dismiss. Once you mess up a shot, you won't make the same mistake again. You discover things by looking back through your work. Some small element might jump out that passed you by initially because your concentration was elsewhere. That's why it's always good to hang on to anything you even have an inkling might have some potential.

The only time I'll import and keep every frame is after a big trip like New York, even when I've done bursts of the same composition. It can be small differences that make one image stronger than another. There might be something behind the subject that doesn't line up quite right. Or, in the case of a silhouette, it might be that the person's head is turning very slightly so they're more directly in profile; frequently with a silhouette, it's that split second when the chin separates from the shoulder. There are sometimes trade-offs, but you have to make a decision and stick with it.

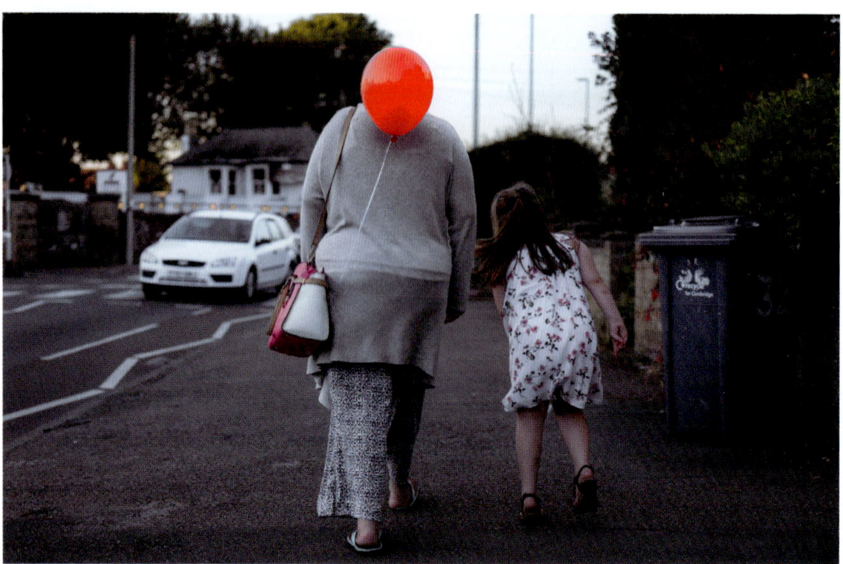

Your photographic style is as much about your selections in the edit as how you shoot. Cambridge, 2018.

Rejected images are often interesting to others, as they give an insight into your creative process – just like a contact sheet in the days of analogue photography. You can find clever ways to share them with your audience. If you've got three or four shots of the same thing and they're all great, stick them in a carousel post on Instagram. People get to see the variations going on when you're shooting. I've shown the 'before' and 'after' shots of the floating hat where you can still see the whole man's torso and the kids on the swing at Tate Modern running through the frame (see pages 95 and 121). It's a nice tool to be able to talk about what works and what doesn't and how I make choices. It can help others to develop their own street photography.

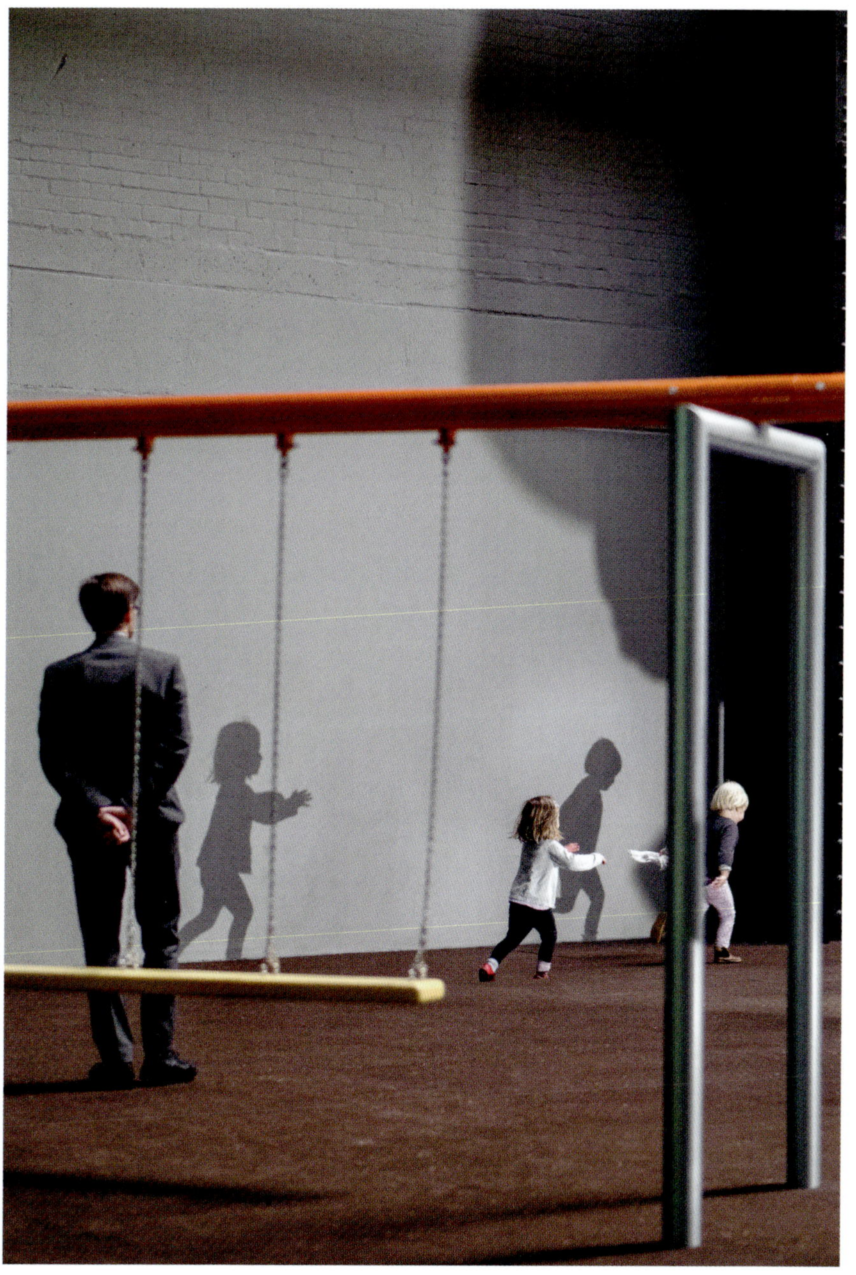

My followers love to see out-takes like this shot of the Tate Modern swing discussed on p.72.
London, 2017

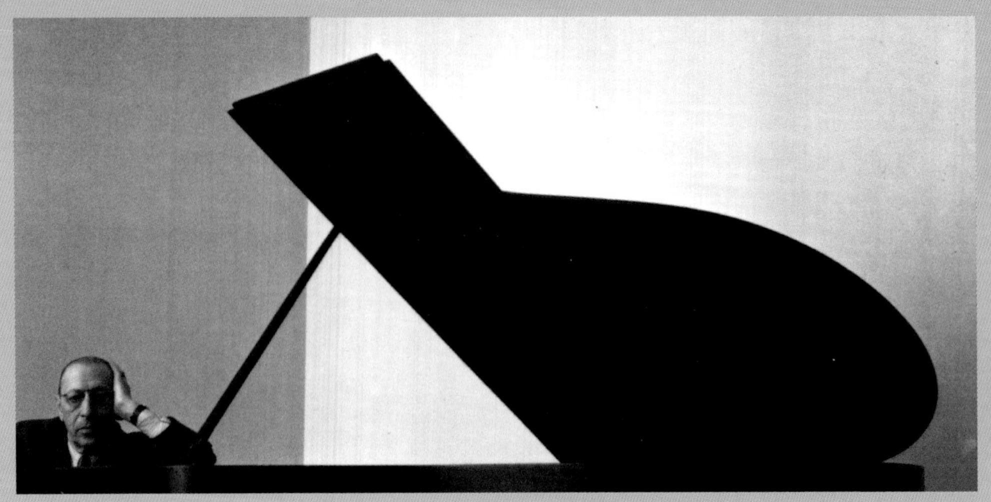

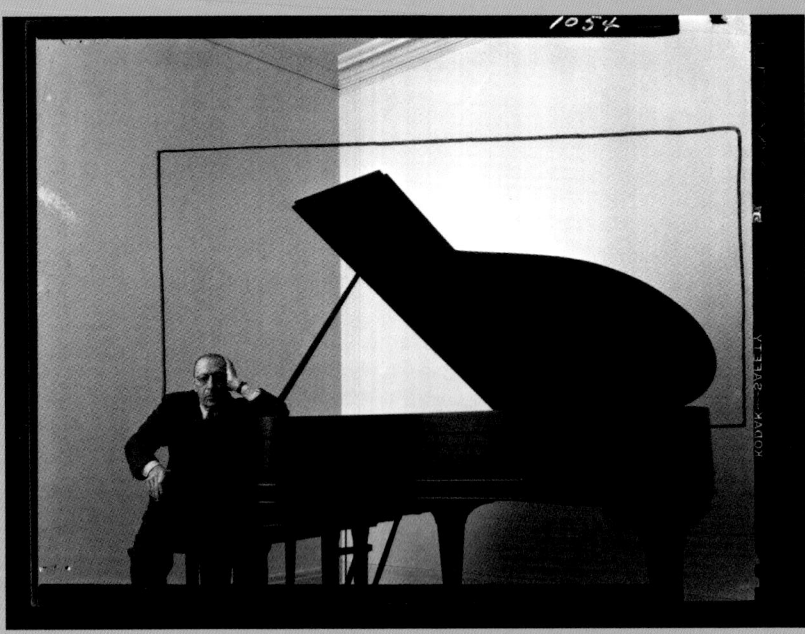

An example I always return to as evidence that cropping is a powerful compositional tool.
© Arnold Newman / Getty Images

18

Let your images shine

Go easy on the post-production – subtle tweaks, made incisively, will bring out the best in your work

American photographer Arnold Newman was renowned for his portraits of musicians and artists and there is a picture of his that has always stayed with me. The success of this image isn't so much about what is included as what is subtracted. It's a portrait of Russian composer and pianist, Igor Stravinsky, with his grand piano. Stravinksy is in the bottom left corner of the frame, head in hand, almost wedged in, while this magnificent great hulking musical instrument takes up almost all the rest of the frame. It's an unconventional composition. You'd assume, with a portrait, that the person would be the most prominent element. But it says something about the intensity of the musician's relationship with his instrument.

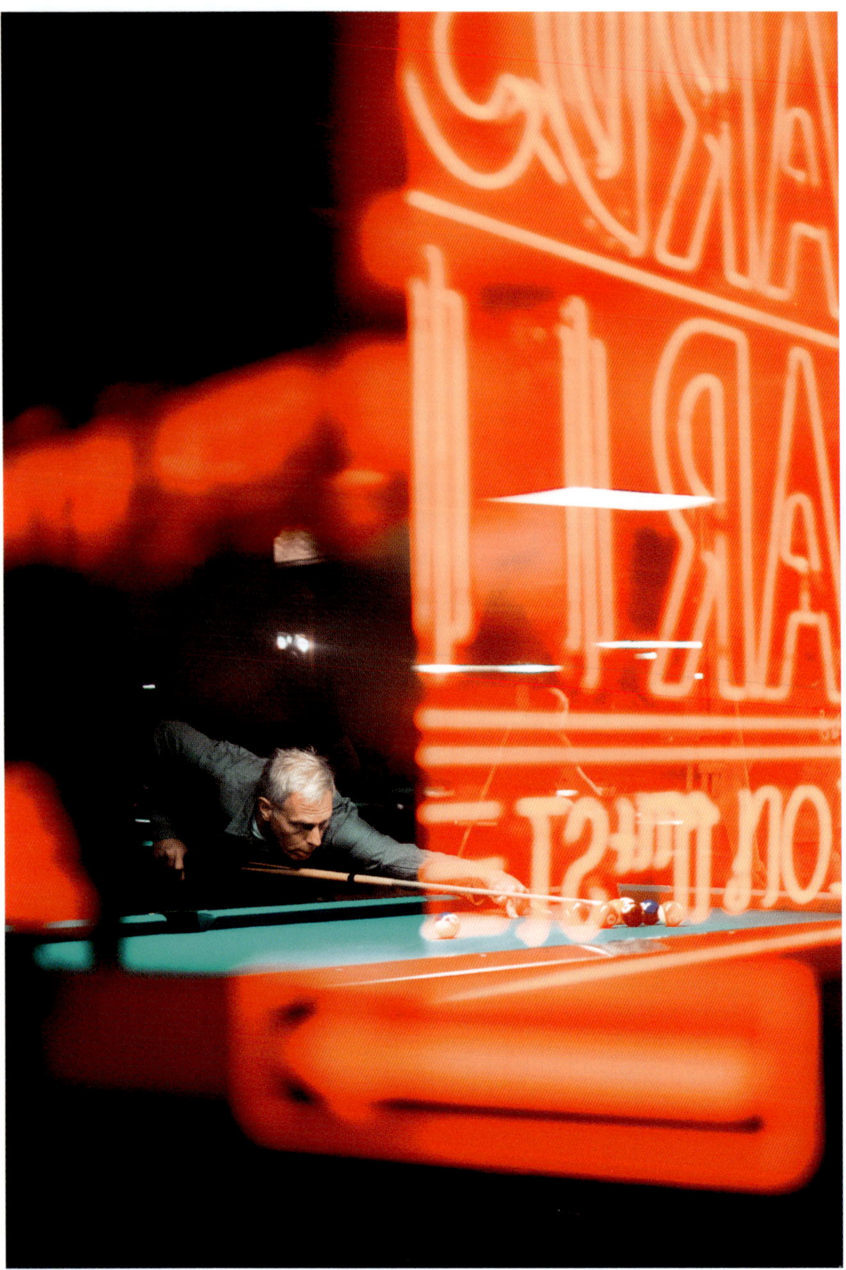

I'll heighten the hue of colours like the red here, making sure that they still look realistic.
New York, 2018

I've seen the original version of this image – a wider shot covered in pencil-drawn crop marks, with the the piano legs in shot. The crop is such a brilliant piece of graphic design, sparse to the point of perfection, taking away all possible elements until what you are left with is total, minimalist clarity. I didn't look at the first version and think, 'Oh, he cropped it, that means it's not so good.' I thought, 'I'm so glad he cropped it.' The result comes first. I follow this ethos when it comes to working with my own images. There are purists out there, street photographers who don't want to edit or crop at all. And I agree to an extent – it's great to try and get it right in-camera as much as you conceivably can. Don't just walk around with a wide-angle lens and crop out compositions from that all the time.

'The main rule that street photographers agree on when it comes to editing is to stay true to the candid element.'

But I also want my images to look their best, and if I can make them slightly cleaner by cropping, I will.

In my Tate Modern image with the kids on the swing (see page 73) there was a black backpack that I excluded with a crop. There was just no need for it to be there. This is a grey area, but I guess the main rule that street photographers agree on when it comes to editing is to stay true to the candid element. Cropping something out is one thing, but actually removing an element from within the frame would be a no-no. Then the image is no longer an accurate representation of something you saw at the time.

However heavily you process your images – and some street photographers do go in for making everything look like a shot from *Blade Runner* – you haven't staged the image. That's the big difference. In my shot of the gent in London who is holding a phone and the facemask hanging off his hand (see page 76), there's a thread of cotton on the back of his jacket. It drives me crazy. I hate it. But I can't remove it. It has to be there. That said, if there is a blemish, and I'm not sure whether it was caused by dust on my sensor or is actually in the shot, it wouldn't bother me to remove it.

I might spend a few minutes at most in post-production, subtly working the colour of each shot. In the early days, I was a little more restrained with colour, but now really punchy colour that still looks natural has become my trademark. When I'm editing, it's important that skin tones still look authentic and that highlights are not too cyan, because that can become obvious. Take this image of a rose on a blue table. I adjusted the yellow to make a more mustard shade because I didn't like the original yellow. In cases like this, you have more freedom to control the colour because no one knows the exact tone of the yellow to begin with. It can be very different when dealing with something well known, such as the shade of red on a can of Coke. Be just as conscious of such elements as you would be with skin tones.

I like warmth; you'll never see that sci-fi look in my images. I also tend to desaturate if there's a blue cast on a white shirt in my shots because I just don't like the look of those blue highlights. Brush up on the basic physics of light, the way colour saturation falls off into shadow – I did this by watching a Photoshop video tutorial years back – and ensure whatever you do to your images is realistic. There's a point where everything can start to look fake. Pull back before you reach it. Keep in mind that images also look brighter on screen compared to print and make sure to embed colour profiles in your images if you're using a good print service. I tend to look at an image on my phone with the brightness down before I post anything, because most people are going to have their phone screens set around that kind of ballpark and I'm always conscious of how the majority of people will see the image. Then I might make some more minor adjustments before sharing to Instagram.

With editing, I have become more open to experimentation. Street photography is something I fell into by circumstance, almost arbitrarily. When I started taking pictures, I decided that was the space I wanted to inhabit because it was most accessible to me at that stage, and some rules have come along because of that. There is a fuzzy border regarding what is an acceptable level of post-processing. There are those who use a really surreal, clearly altered colour palette and are still considered street photographers. For me, that's too far. But at the same time, it's something I'm always internally wrestling with as I consider whether I always want to be a street photographer or would I rather just be a photographer?

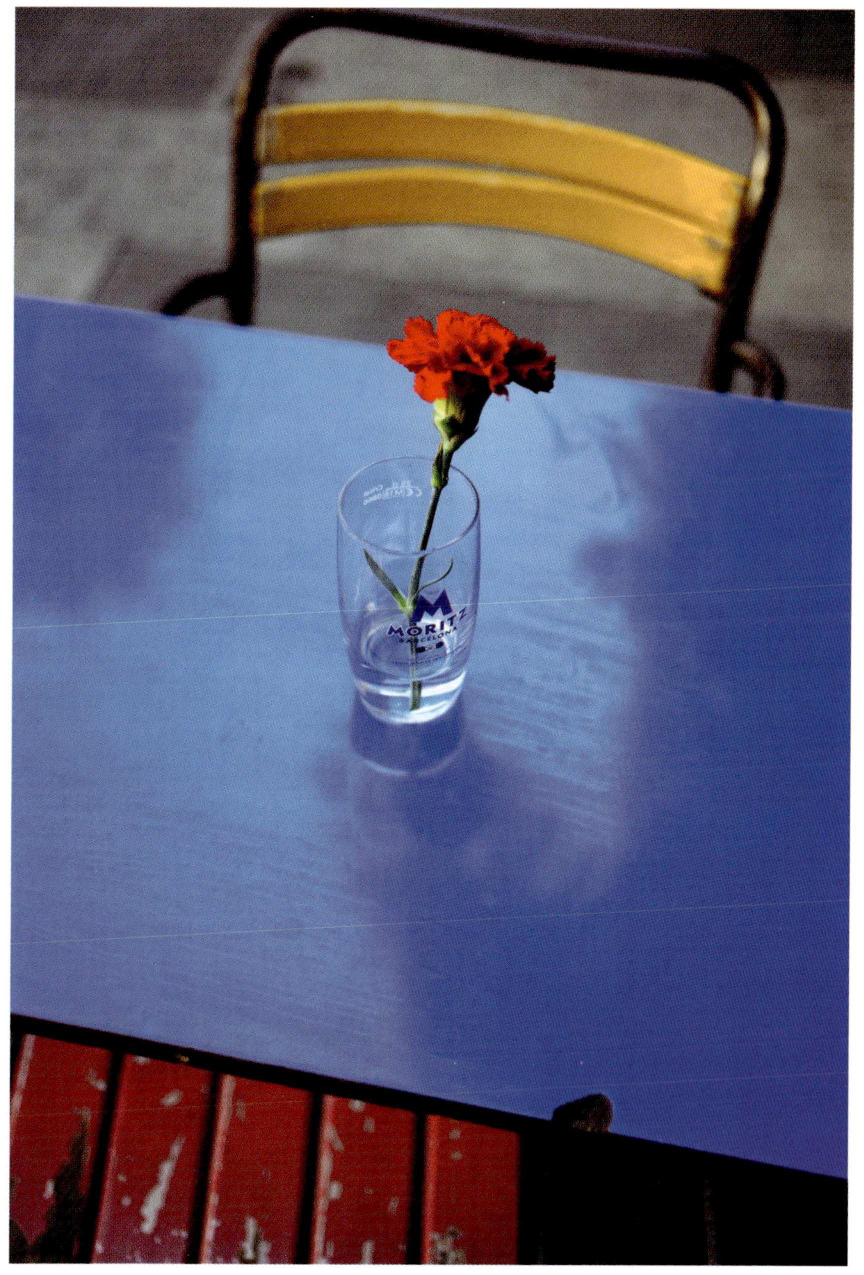

Remember smartphone screens enhance brightness when processing vivid images like this.
Barcelona, 2019

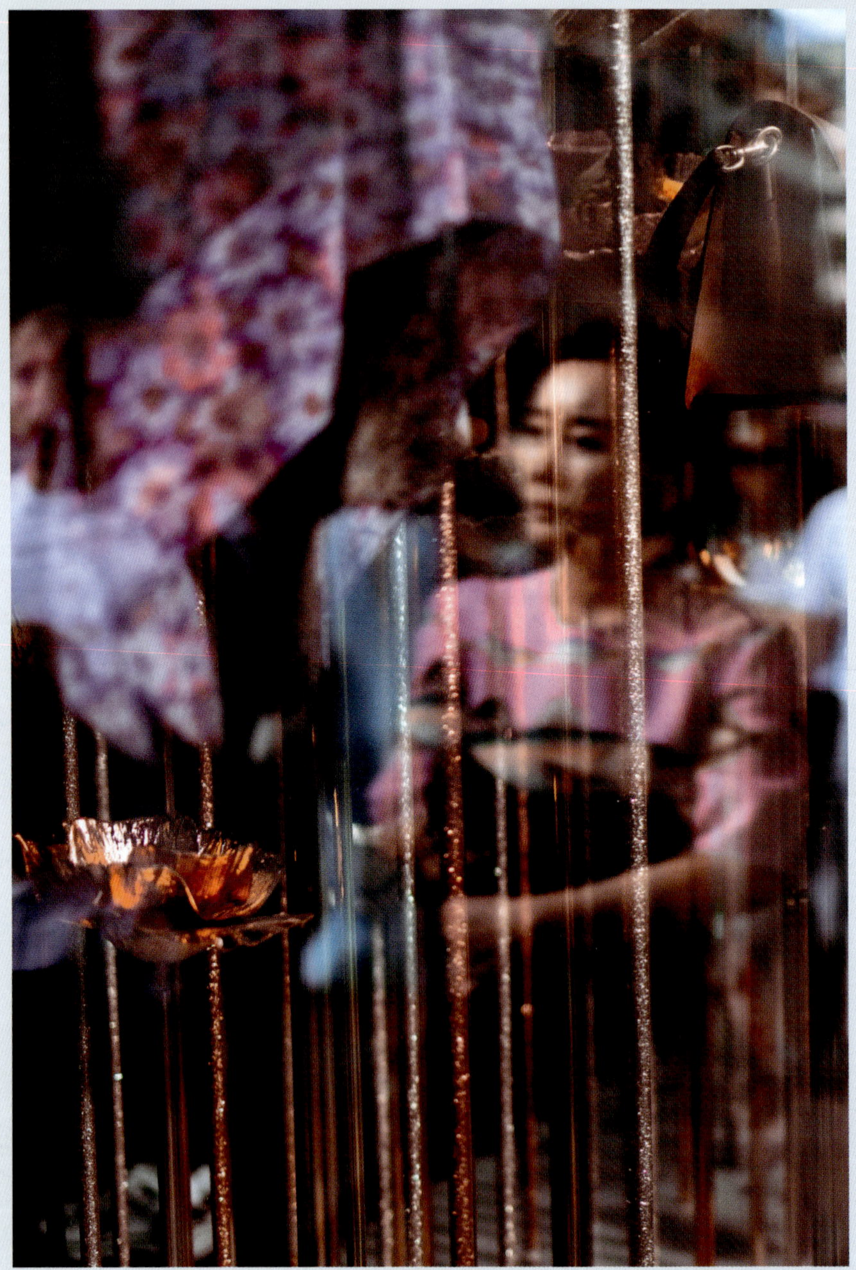

Don't let social media success stop you evolving creatively. Otherwise, what's the point?
London, 2019

19

Pop the Insta bubble

Nothing beats social for some things – but don't get caught up in it

Without Instagram, my street photography story would have been very different. I never would have connected with people like Ted Forbes and Kai Wong or appeared on Wong's YouTube channel. I never would have had Skillshare classes, I never would have been able to self-publish a book, entitled *New York*, of my work in the city. None of those things would have been possible. There is a balance to be struck. Social media can create a network that supports you, inspires you and presents you with new opportunities. It can expose your work to audiences of hundreds of thousands of followers, giving you a profile that will take you places. But success on Instagram also brings certain expectations, pressures and limitations.

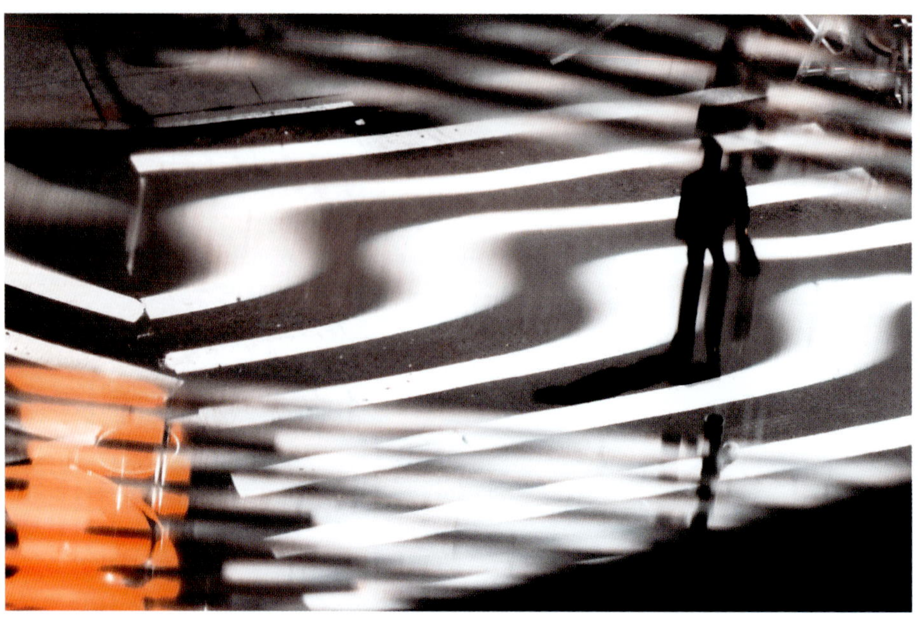

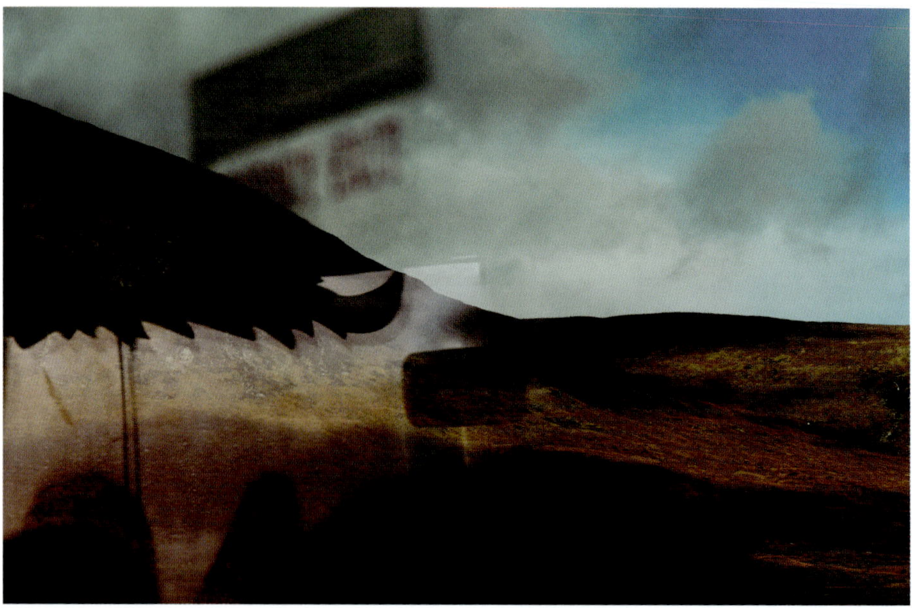

More subtle images like these aren't always an instant hit, so they won't be seen as widely.
ABOVE New York, 2019
BELOW Scotland, 2022

I joined Instagram in 2016 and I feel like I arrived late. There was a whole bunch of accounts that were way bigger than mine when I was starting to push my work out. But I'm very grateful that I got to it when I did, because I have no idea how you'd grow an account successfully now. When everything you posted simply appeared chronologically, it was a motivator. You had to put new images out every day and if they were good, they would get traction. Back then, if you posted at a particular time, you knew that was when people would see your image. Now, you have no idea.

The reason for this is the ever-changing Instagram algorithm – the set of rules that determines when and how your content will be seen. At the time of writing, photographers have noticed the algorithm prioritises reels and videos over stills. I don't want to be forced to create content in a different way. I don't want to suddenly become a videographer. As cool as some of that type of work is, that's not what I do. So, instead, it's about finding ways to reformat the material I've already got. You can have a lot of success putting still images into reels and playing around with that or creating a 15-second video of a still image. In your feed, it looks no different.

When you do post a single, still image, it will initially get shown to a small number of your followers and if it doesn't get a positive response straight away, it won't be shared further, so hardly anyone gets to see it. That means that images that are more subtle or niche won't get a fair chance to be seen compared to more obvious crowd-pleaser. This 100 per cent affects the type of images that people shoot and share. How could it not? And that, in turn, creates a kind of echo chamber where everyone is photographing in a similar way. Pandering to the algorithm is a hard habit to break. One impact of this is that we all shoot in portrait orientation because social media favours that, even though some of the best early street photographers shot amazing landscape images. As you realise what's successful, you shoot more of that and the images that the algorithm shows you reflect and reinforce that, especially if you've got a bigger account. So, it just goes round and round.

'Social media can create a network that supports you, inspires you and presents you with new opportunities.'

Often, the images that have the biggest draw on social media aren't the ones I like best, but I share them because I think they'll go down well. There's one I shot in Regent Street, London, with some buildings reflected in it and a silhouette in the bottom left. I was doing a tutorial with someone, demonstrating how I would compose a scene by lining up some steps with a window ledge. There's nothing wrong with it, but it just seems so obvious to me. It's always been really popular on social media, but if you made me pick out my 20 best photos, it's not going to be in there. It's important for me to step outside the social media bubble and remind myself that I have the freedom to post something weird that I really like. In a way, that's an unforeseen advantage of the algorithm being less predictable because it is always being fine-tuned and isn't simply based on the time of posting, so growth is trickier to control – it's kind of liberating. Some people are just ignoring the algorithm altogether now. It's also worth remembering that an image that works well on Instagram isn't always going to be one that works well in print. A scene that is bigger, with greater complexity can get lost on the pocket-sized screen of a smartphone, for example. There are shots that I hold back, knowing they won't have that instant impact, but would look really good in a book or on a gallery wall.

Quite often, the photographers whose work I respect most – the people who are doing commissions and editorial for brands that I like – don't necessarily do that well on social media, even though their images are incredible. It takes a lot longer to find them but when I do, I'm just hooked. And I'll seek such work out. I won't wait expectantly for the algorithm to serve it up in my feed, I'll go in and check a photographer's account regularly. And the more 'weird' pictures that I've been taking lately have led to bigger jobs and bigger deals than I ever had when I was pandering to the algorithm. The only time I'll play the game now is if I'm making sponsored content, which is more likely to be formatted as a reel anyway. If having a bigger account brings pressure, it also has the benefit of not having to worry about trying to build it through each individual image to bring in new followers. I can just do whatever I want.

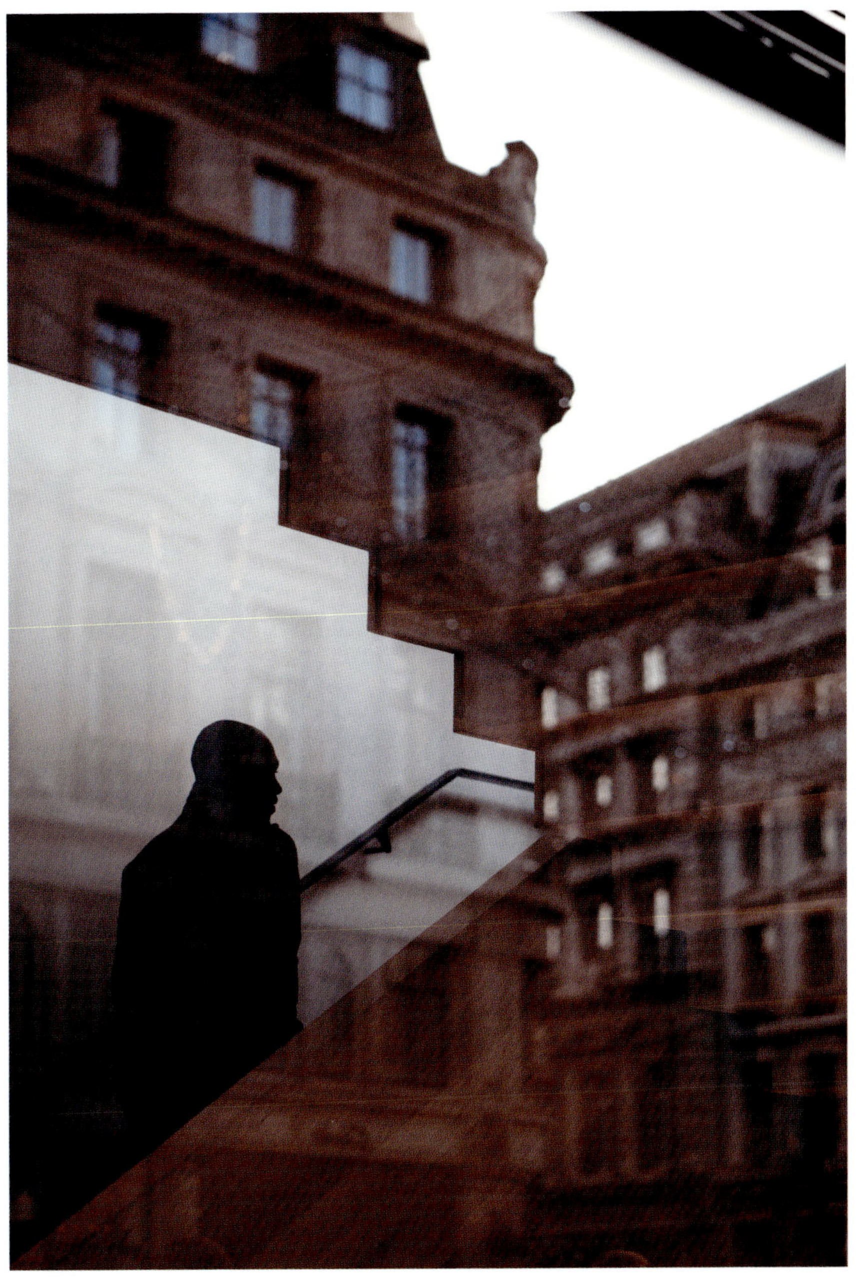

Some shots I take knowing they will be crowd-pleasers on social. It's about finding a balance.
London, 2017

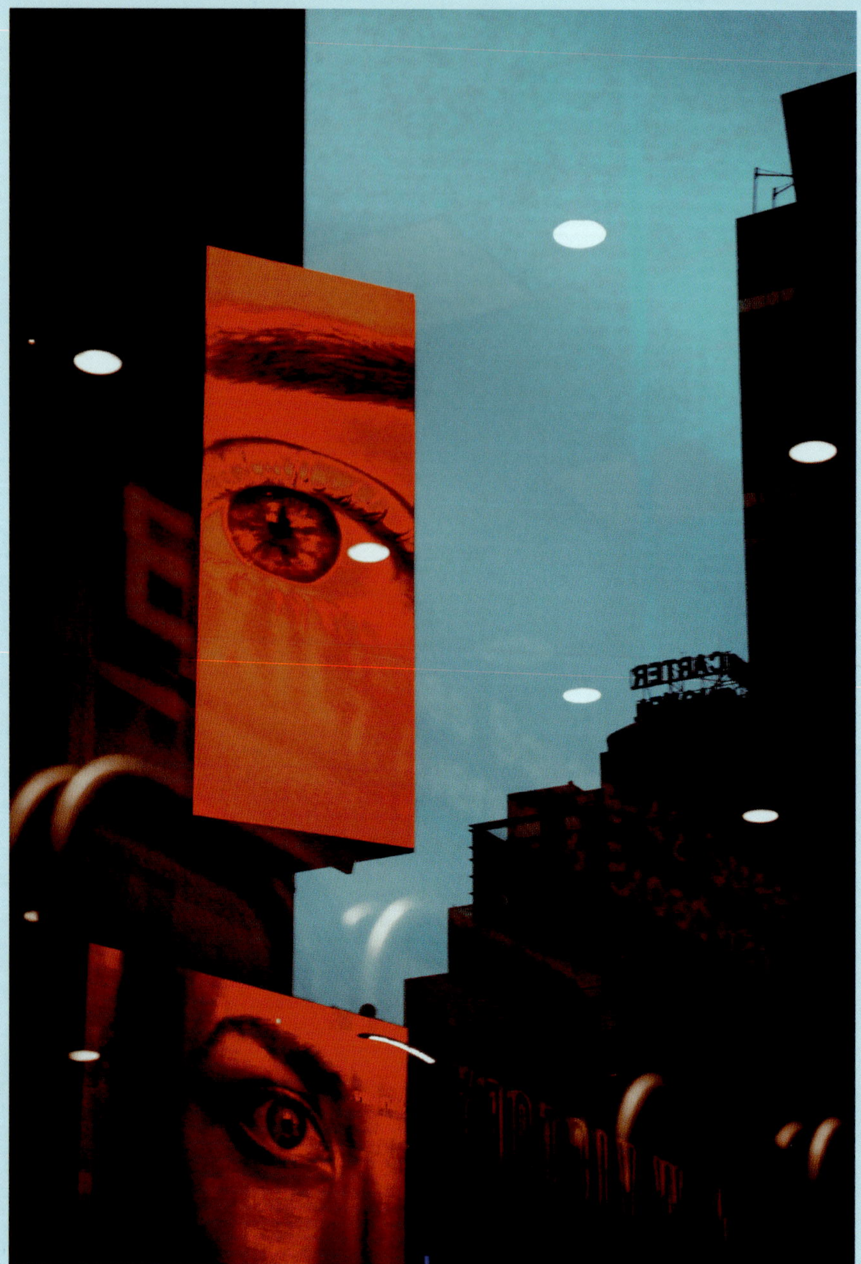

My inspiration will always be the painterly street photographers of New York. I just love colour.
New York, 2022

20

Stay curious

Keep your eyes open – inspiration is everywhere

Every street photographer goes on a journey. I started mine in a completely different place to where I am now. I thought I knew what street photography was – fast-paced and in-your-face, but that wasn't really me. When I discovered the painterly style of Saul Leiter and Ernst Haas, it felt like a homecoming. Leiter once famously said, 'A window covered with raindrops interests me more than a photograph of a famous person.' I couldn't agree more.

As my work has developed, colour is one of the things I've become best known for and that has shaped the way I see and shoot. Having a consistent visual style is what gives your photography an authorial stamp and keeps people coming back for more. It's also restricted me, in some ways. More recently, I have discovered photographers like Jack Davison, whose work I absolutely love and who shoots colour or monochrome, depending on what fits the scene. I've always been an admirer of Sebastião Salgado, who works exclusively in black and white, as well as Arnold Newman and Ralph Gibson, who produced sleek, graphical compositions. I've started

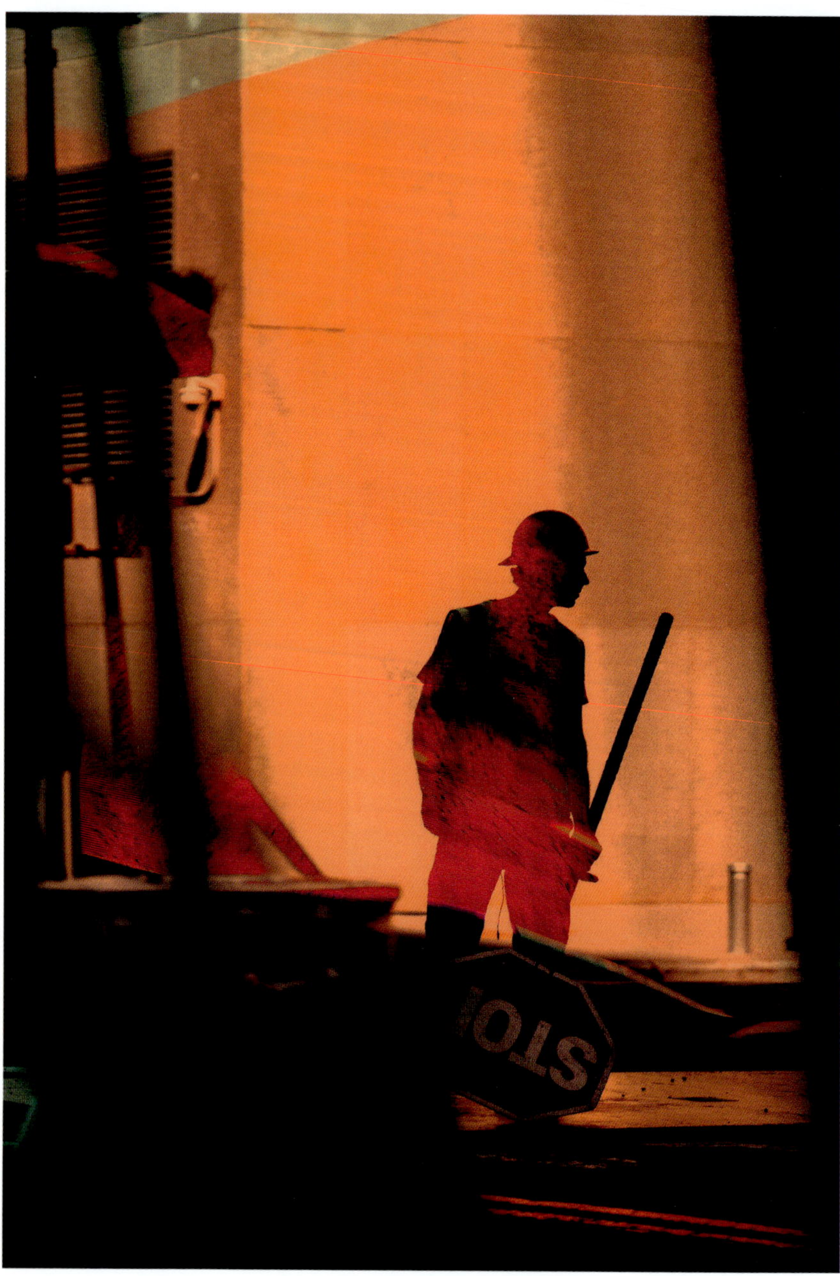

Colour photography is what I'm known for, but that hasn't stopped me exploring monochrome.
ABOVE New York, 2022
RIGHT Cambridge, 2020

to wonder, 'Why am I so fixated on only shooting in colour? Does it matter?'

The conundrum of social media is that when you start to earn a reputation, there's a fear of doing something different. But you only have to look at the great photographers of the past to see that this is misplaced. Take Harry Gruyaert. He is a Magnum photographer, noted for his colour documentary work in India and North Africa, but he also shot fashion for Hermès. The work is different from what he shot on the street, but it's still him and completely different from what your average fashion photographer would do. You can evolve, and as long as the change doesn't feel too abrupt, your followers will come along with you. In the last few months, I've started throwing in some more unorthodox shots that people might not expect, like composite work or images based around daily life like this picture of a New York workman, which brings in light and texture to give it a different mood to what you expect from street photos. I've also shared images from my exploration of monochrome, some of which are the opposite – figurative to the point of portraiture – like this image of a man with one eye concealed with a circular blast of light.

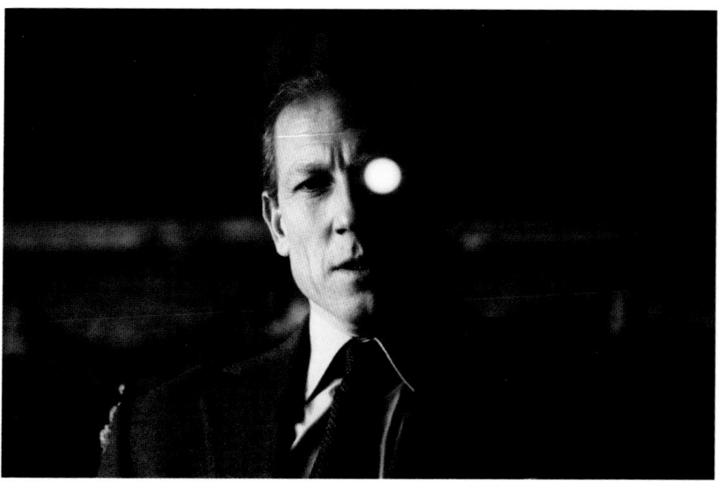

Increasingly, I'm embracing a more experimental approach. I'm giving myself greater freedom, even if that means not sticking to the strict label of 'street photographer'. I'm just thinking of myself as a 'photographer'. These days, I like to set myself new challenges, like seeing what happens if I subject my street images to a strange, warping effect in Photoshop. I'm also exploring ways to do that in-camera, using an acrylic mirror that I manipulate with my hands and re-photographing an image I've taken reflected from my laptop screen into that mirror. Trying to do these things manually rather than in post-production is just more interesting to me, and more challenging and more confusing for people looking at the final image.

In order to improve, you have to try new things and expect to take some terrible photos. Switching up lenses changes the way you look at everything. Using a macro lens on the street would be very odd, for example, but would force some creative usage that might lead to something that really stands out. Revisiting your archive can send you down unforeseen paths. There might be a throwaway shot that suddenly speaks to you. Maybe you notice some abstraction, a reflection or colour that passed you by first time around. Return to some of the places where you've shot previously, but employ a new method or add an extra layer of distortion and see how that changes things. Keep adding more complexity to the process. Get your hands on texture people aren't used to seeing – go to thrift stores and find old glass ashtrays with bizarre shapes that distort things. Try shooting through one of those.

Often, I try to reverse-engineer someone else's setup, and in that process I'll stumble across another way of doing things. Inspiration can come from anywhere. I'm also always looking at influences from outside of photography – at the work of illustrator, David Foldvari, for example. I always heard that the texture in his early images was created by photocopying his drawings. Anyone who's ever been handed a test in school that includes a colour diagram will be familiar with the degraded look of the image. There's no reason why you can't replicate that digitally. Take a

'Don't play it safe, don't be constrained by genres, rules or labels, but experiment as much as you can until you hit on something you really love.'

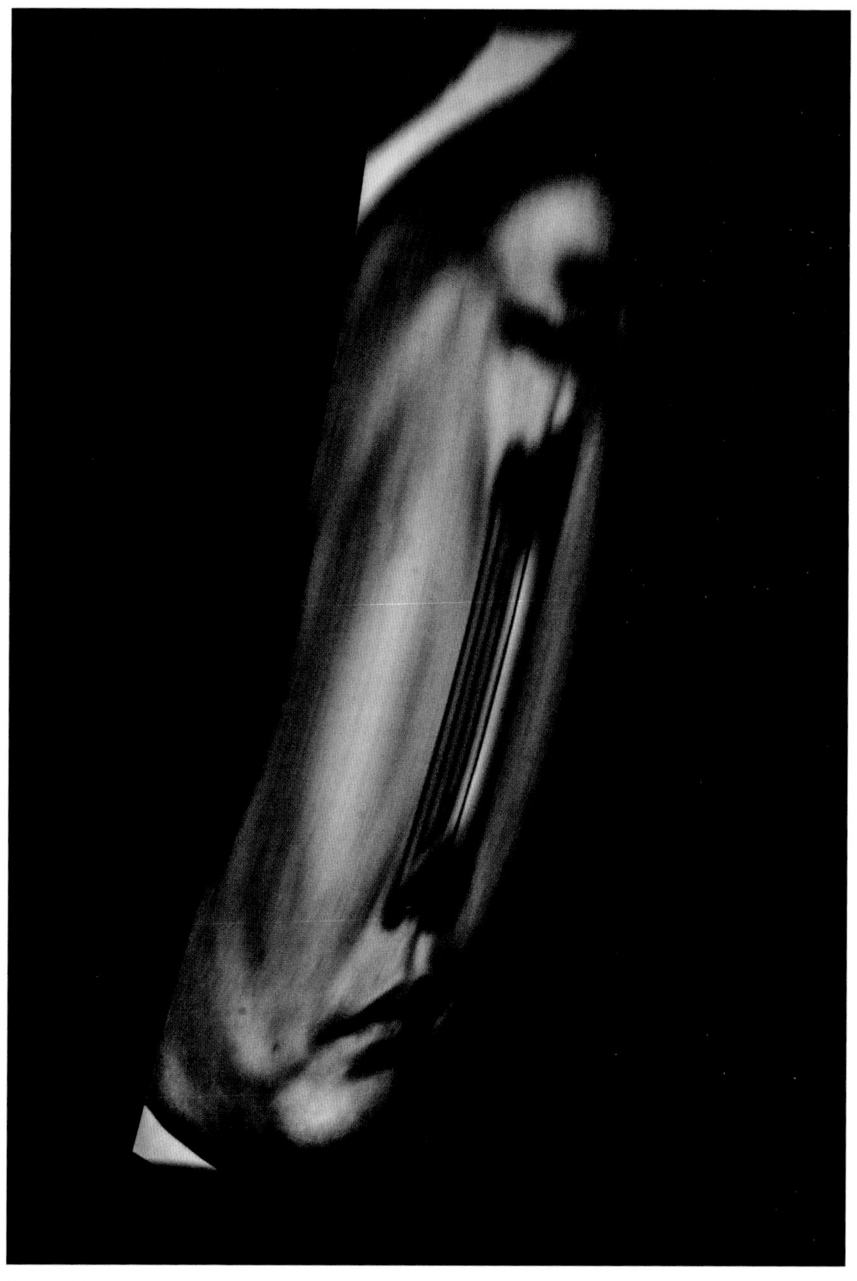

Keep pushing yourself to try out things. This image isn't anything like you'd expect from me.
Cambridge, 2022

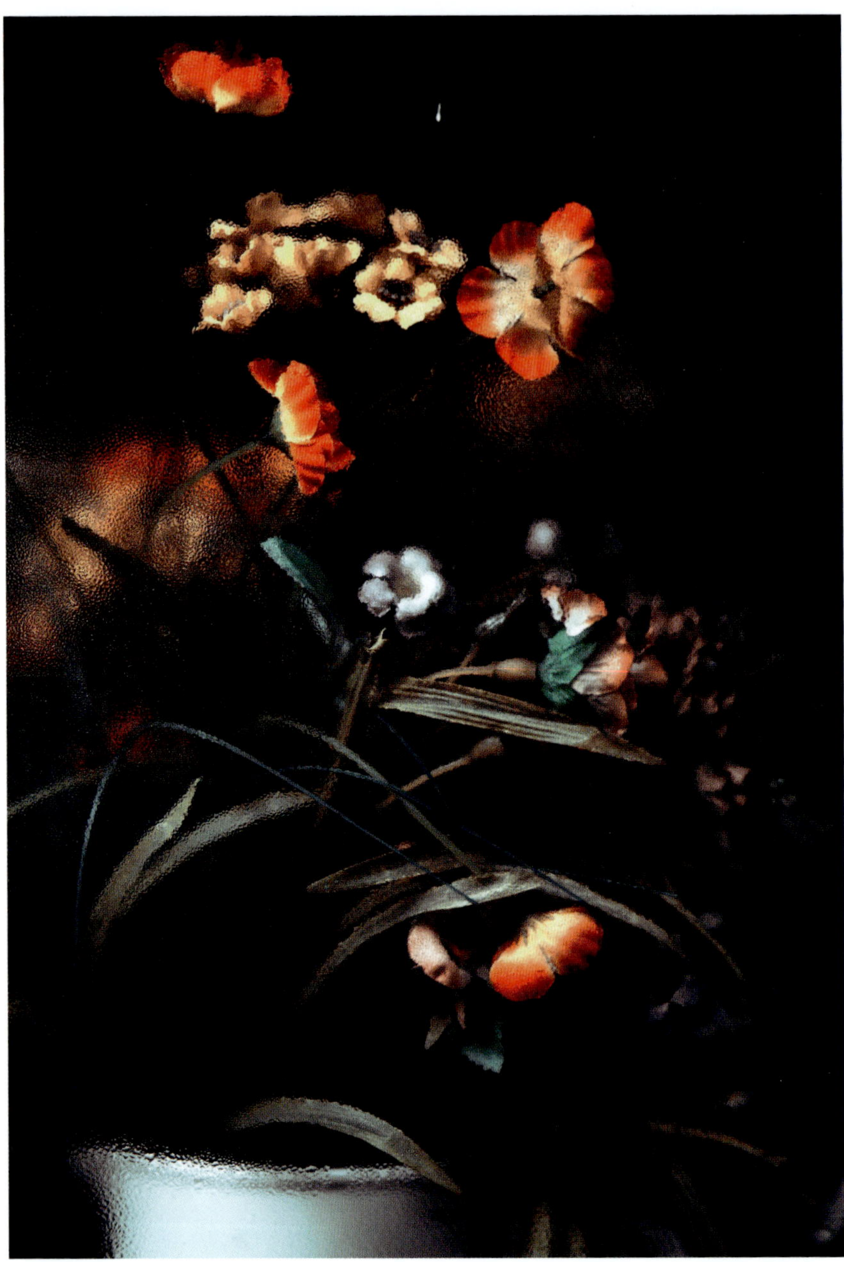

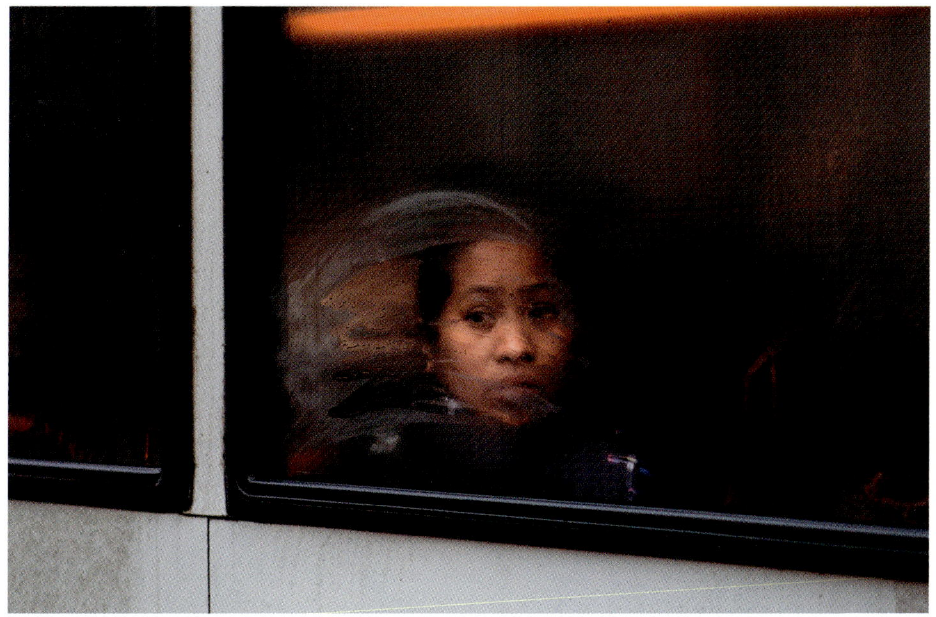

screenshot, then upload it and screenshot that. Upload it again, and so on, or make a print of your work and see how photocopying a colour image in black and white alters it.

Compared to some people, I've been a photographer for a long time, but in some ways I'm just getting started. I'm grateful for the success and the opportunities I've had so far, but I don't want just to stick to what I've done already. And nor should you. So, don't play it safe, don't be constrained by genres, rules or labels, but experiment as much as you can until you hit on something you really love – whether that's on the streets or somewhere else. If, like me, you are someone who is more driven by visual aesthetic than random human interaction, there is no limit to where your own street photography journey will take you – enjoy the ride. This might be an odd thing to read at the end of a book about street photography, but you don't have to be a street photographer. Just be weird. Figure out how to do the things the people you admire do. And then do something they never would have thought of.

Index

Page numbers in *italics*
refer to illustrations

Quarto

First published in 2023 by Frances Lincoln,
an imprint of The Quarto Group.
One Triptych Place, London, SE1 9SH
United Kingdom
T (0)20 7700 9000
www.Quarto.com

EEA Representation, WTS Tax d.o.o., Žanova ulica
3, 4000 Kranj, Slovenia.
www.wts-tax.si

A catalogue record for this book is available
from the British Library.

ISBN 978-0-7112-8363-3
Ebook ISBN 978-0-7112-8364-0

10 9 8 7

Design by Claire Warner Studio
Editorial research by Rachel Segal Hamilton

Printed in Huizhou, Guangdong, China, TT032026

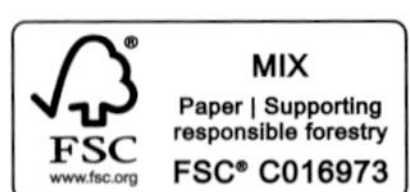